INVESTMENT ANALYSIS AND PORTFOLIO MANAGEMENT ARVIND CAPITALS

ARVIND UPADHYAY

Investment analysis and portfolio management book objective is to help entrepreneurs and practitioners to understand the investments field as it is currently understood and practiced for sound investment decisions making. Following this objective, key concepts are presented to provide an appreciation of the theory and practice of investments, focusing on investment portfolio formation and management issues. This course is designed to emphasize both theoretical and analytical aspects of investment decisions and deals with modern investment theoretical concepts and instruments. Both descriptive and quantitative materials on investing are presented. Upon completion of this course the entrepreneurs shall be able: • to describe and to analyze the investment environment, different types of investment vehicles; • to understand and to explain the logic of investment process and the contents of its' each stage; • to use the quantitative methods for investment decision making – to calculate risk and expected return of various investment tools and the investment portfolio; • to distinguish concepts of portfolio theory and apply its' principals in the process of investment portfolio formation; • to analyze and to evaluate relevance of stocks, bonds, options for the investments; • to understand the psychological issues in investment decision making; • to know active and passive investment strategies and to apply them in practice.

As has been mentioned before, every chapter of the book contains opportunities to test the knowledge of the audience, which are in the form of questions and more involved problems. The types of question include open ended questions as well as multiple choice questions. The problems usually involve calculations using quantitative tools of investment analysis, analysis of various types of securities, finding and discussing the alternatives for investment decision making.

The book provides the target audience with a broad knowledge on the key topics of investment analysis and management. book emphasizes both theoretical and analytical aspects of investment decision making, analysis and evaluation of different corporate securities as investments, portfolio diversification and management. Special attention is given to the formulation of investment policy and strategy.

Investing versus financing

The term 'investing" could be associated with the different activities, but the common target in these activities is to "employ" the money (funds) during the time period seeking to enhance the investor's wealth. Funds to be invested come from assets already owned, borrowed money and savings. By foregoing consumption today and investing their savings, investors expect to enhance their future consumption possibilities by increasing their wealth. But it is useful to make a distinction between real and financial investments. Real investments generally involve some kind of tangible asset, such as land, machinery, factories, etc. Financial investments involve contracts in paper or electronic form such as stocks, bonds, etc. Following the objective as it presented in the introduction this course deals only with the financial investments because the key theoretical investment concepts and portfolio theory are based on these investments and allow to analyze investment process and investment management decision making in the substantially broader context Some information presented in some chapters of this material developed for the investments course could be familiar for those who have studied other courses in finance, particularly corporate finance. Corporate finance typically covers such issues as capital structure, short-term and long-term financing, project analysis, current asset management. Capital structure addresses the question of what type of long-term financing is the best for the company under current and forecasted market conditions; project analysis is concerned with the determining whether a project should be undertaken. Current assets and current liabilities management addresses how to manage the day-by-day cash flows of the firm. Corporate finance is also concerned with how to allocate the profit of the firm among shareholders (through the dividend payments), the government (through tax payments) and the firm itself (through retained earnings). But one of the most important questions for the company is financing. Modern firms raise money by issuing stocks and bonds. These securities are traded in the financial markets and the investors have possibility to buy or to sell securities issued by the companies. Thus, the investors and companies, searching for financing, realize their interest in the same place – in financial markets. Corporate finance area of studies and practice involves the interaction between firms and financial markets and Investments area of studies and practice involves the interaction between investors and financial markets. Investments field also differ from the corporate finance in using the relevant methods for research and decision making. Investment problems in many cases allow for a quantitative analysis and modeling approach and the qualitative methods together with quantitative methods are more often used analyzing corporate finance problems. The other very important difference is, that investment analysis for decision making can be based on the large data sets available form the financial markets, such as stock returns, thus, the mathematical statistics methods can be used. But at the same time both Corporate Finance and Investments are built upon a common set of financial principles, such as the present value, the future value, the cost of capital). And very often investment and financing analysis for decision making use the same tools, but the interpretation of the results from this analysis for the investor and for the financier would be different. For example, when issuing the securities and selling them in the market the company perform valuation looking for the higher price and for the lower cost of capital, but the investor using valuation search for attractive securities with the lower price and the higher possible required rate of return on his/ her investments. Together with the investment the term speculation is frequently used. Speculation can be described as investment too, but it is related with the short-term investment horizons and usually involves purchasing the salable securities with the hope that its price will increase rapidly, providing a quick profit. Speculators try to buy low and to sell high, their primary concern is with anticipating and profiting from market fluctuations. But as the fluctuations in the financial markets are and become more and more unpredictable speculations are treated as the investments of highest risk. In contrast, an investment is based upon the analysis and its main goal is to promise safety of principle sum invested and to earn the satisfactory risk.

There are two types of investors:

individual investors;

Institutional investors.

Individual investors are individuals who are investing on their own. Sometimes individual investors are called retail investors. Institutional investors are entities such as investment companies, commercial banks, insurance companies, pension funds and other financial institutions. In recent years the process of institutionalization of investors can be observed. As the main reasons for this can be mentioned the fact, that institutional investors can achieve economies of scale, demographic pressure on social security, the changing role of banks. One of important preconditions for successful investing both for individual and institutional investors is the favorable investment environment . Our focus in developing this course is on the management of individual investors' portfolios. But the basic principles of investment management are applicable both for individual and institutional investors.

Direct versus indirect investing

Investors can use direct or indirect type of investing. Direct investing is realized using financial markets and indirect investing involves financial intermediaries. The primary *difference between these two types of investing is that applying direct investing investors buy and sell financial assets and manage individual investment portfolio themselves. Consequently, investing directly through financial markets investors take all the risk and their successful investing depends on their understanding of financial markets, its fluctuations and on their abilities to analyze and to evaluate the investments and to manage their investment portfolio. Contrary, using indirect type of investing investors are buying or selling financial instruments of financial intermediaries (financial institutions) which invest large pools of funds in the financial markets and hold portfolios. Indirect investing relieves investors from making decisions about their portfolio. As shareholders with the ownership interest in the portfolios managed by financial institutions (investment companies, pension funds, insurance companies, commercial banks) the investors are entitled to their share of dividends, interest and capital gains generated and pay their share of the institution's expenses and portfolio management fee. The risk for investor using indirect investing is related more with the credibility of chosen institution and the professionalism of portfolio managers. In general, indirect investing is more related with the financial institutions which are primarily in the business of investing in and managing a portfolio of securities (various types of investment funds or investment companies, private pension funds). By pooling the funds of thousands of investors, those companies can offer them a variety of services, in addition to diversification, including professional management of their financial assets and liquidity. Investors can "employ" their funds by performing direct transactions, bypassing both financial institutions and financial markets (for example, direct lending). But such transactions are very risky, if a large amount of money is transferred only to one's hands, following the well known American proverb "don't put all your eggs in one basket" (Cambridge Idioms Dictionary, 2nd ed. Cambridge University Press 2006). That turns to the necessity to diversify your investments. From the other side, direct transactions in the businesses are strictly limited by laws avoiding possibility of money laundering.*

Types of investing and alternatives for financing

Types of investing in the economy

Alternatives for financing in the economy Direct investing (through financial markets) Raising equity capital or borrowing in financial markets Indirect investing (through financial institutions) Borrowing from financial institutions Direct transactions Direct borrowing, partnership contracts members by or sell for their own account, functioning as dealers or market makers who set prices at which they are willing to buy and sell for their own account. Exchanges play very important role in the modern economies by performing the following tasks: • Supervision of trading to ensure fairness and efficiency; • The authorization and regulation of market participants such as brokers and market makers; • Creation of an environment in which securities' prices are formed efficiently and without distortion. This requires not only regulation of an orders and transaction costs but also a liquid market in which there are many buyers and sellers, allowing investors to buy or to sell their securities quickly; • Organization of the clearing and settlement of transactions; • The regulation of he admission of companies to be listed on the exchange and the regulation of companies who are listed on the exchange; • The dissemination of information (trading data, prices and announcements of companies listed on the exchange). Investors are more willing to trade if prompt and complete information about trades and prices in the market is available. The over-the-counter (OTC) market is not a formal exchange. It is organized network of brokers and dealers who negotiate sales of securities. There are no membership requirements and many brokers register as dealers on the OTC. At the same time there are no listing requirements and thousands of securities are traded in the OTC market. OTC stocks are usually considered as very risky because they are the stocks that are not considered large or stable enough to trade on the major exchange. An alternative trading system (ATS) is an electronic trading mechanism developed independently from the established market places – security exchanges – and designed to match buyers and sellers of securities on an agency basis. The brokers who use ATS are acting on behalf of their clients and do not trade on their own account. The distinct advantages of ATS in comparison with traditional markets are cost savings of transactions, the short time of execution of transactions for liquid securities, extended hours for trading and anonymity, often important for investors, trading large amounts. By term of circulation of financial assets traded in the market:

<u>Money market;</u>

<u>Capital market</u>

Money market - in which only short-term financial instruments are traded. Capital market - in which only long-term financial instruments are traded. The capital markets allow firms, governments to finance spending in excess of their current incomes.

Companies can obtain necessary funds directly from the general public (those who have excess money to invest) by the use of the financial market, issuing and selling their securities. Alternatively, they can obtain funds indirectly from the general public by using financial intermediaries. And the intermediaries acquire funds by allowing the general public to maintain such investments as savings accounts, Certificates of deposit accounts and other similar vehicles.

Investment environment

Investment environment can be defined as the existing investment vehicles in the market available for investor and the places for transactions with these investment vehicles. Thus further in this subchapter the main types of investment vehicles and the types of financial markets will be presented and described.

Investment vehicles

we are focused to the financial investments that mean the object will be financial assets and the marketable securities in particular. But even if further in this course only the investments in financial assets are discussed, for deeper understanding the specifics of financial assets comparison of some important characteristics of investment in this type of assets with the investment in physical assets is presented. Investment in financial assets differs from investment in physical assets in those important aspects: • Financial assets are divisible, whereas most physical assets are not. An asset is divisible if investor can buy or sell small portion of it. In case of financial assets it means, that investor, for example, can buy or sell a small fraction of the whole company as investment object buying or selling a number of common stocks. • Marketability (or Liquidity) is a characteristic of financial assets that is not shared by physical assets, which usually have low liquidity. Marketability (or liquidity) reflects the feasibility of converting of the asset into cash quickly and without affecting its price significantly. Most of financial assets are easy to buy or to sell in the financial markets. • The planned holding period of financial assets can be much shorter than the holding period of most physical assets. The holding period for investments is defined as the time between signing a purchasing order for asset and selling the asset. Investors acquiring physical asset usually plan to hold it for a long period, but investing in financial assets, such as securities, even for some months or a year can be reasonable. Holding period for investing in financial assets vary in very wide interval and depends on the investor's goals and investment strategy.

Information about financial assets is often more abundant and less costly to obtain, than information about physical assets. Information availability shows the real possibility of the investors to receive the necessary information which could influence their investment decisions and investment results. Since a big portion of information important for investors in such financial assets as stocks, bonds is publicly available, the impact of many disclosed factors having influence on value of these securities can be included in the analysis and the decisions made by investors. Even if we analyze only financial investment there is a big variety of financial investment vehicles. The on going processes of globalization and integration open wider possibilities for the investors to invest into new investment vehicles which were unavailable for them some time ago because of the weak domestic financial systems and limited technologies for investment in global investment environment. Financial innovations suggest for the investors the new choices of investment but at the same time make the investment process and investment decisions more complicated, because even if the investors have a wide range of alternatives to invest they can't forgot the key rule in investments: invest only in what you really understand. Thus the investor must understand how investment vehicles differ from each other and only then to pick those which best match his/her expectations.

The most important characteristics of investment vehicles on which bases the overall variety of investment vehicles can be assorted are the return on investment and the risk which is defined as the uncertainty about the actual return that will be earned on an investment . Each type of investment vehicles could be characterized by certain level of profitability and risk because of the specifics of these financial instruments. Though all different types of investment vehicles can be compared using characteristics of risk and return and the most risky as well as less risky investment vehicles can be defined. However the risk and return on investment are close related and only using both important characteristics we can really understand the differences in investment vehicles .

The main types of financial investment vehicles are:

- Short term investment vehicles;
- Fixed-income securities;
- Common stock;

• Speculative investment vehicles;

• Other investment tools.

Short - term investment vehicles are all those which have a maturity of one year or less. Short term investment vehicles often are defined as money-market instruments, because they are traded in the money market which presents the financial market for short term (up to one year of maturity) marketable financial assets. The risk as well as the return on investments of short-term investment vehicles usually is lower than for other types of investments. The main short term investment vehicles are: • Certificates of deposit; • Treasury bills; • Commercial paper; • Bankers' acceptances; • Repurchase agreements. Certificate of deposit is debt instrument issued by bank that indicates a specified sum of money has been deposited at the issuing depository institution. Certificate of deposit bears a maturity date and specified interest rate and can be issued in any denomination. Most certificates of deposit cannot be traded and they incur penalties for early withdrawal. For large money-market investors financial institutions allow their large-denomination certificates of deposits to be traded as negotiable certificates of deposits. Treasury bills (also called T-bills) are securities representing financial obligations of the government. Treasury bills have maturities of less than one year. They have the unique feature of being issued at a discount from their nominal value and the difference between nominal value and discount price is the only sum which is paid at the maturity for these short term securities because the interest is not paid in cash, only accrued. The other important feature of T-bills is that they are treated as risk-free securities ignoring inflation and default of a government, which was rare in developed countries, the T-bill will pay the fixed stated yield with certainty. But, of course, the yield on T-bills changes over time influenced by changes in overall macroeconomic situation. T-bills are issued on an auction basis. The issuer accepts competitive bids and allocates bills to those offering the highest prices. Noncompetitive bid is an offer to purchase the bills at a price that equals the average of the competitive bids. Bills can be traded before the maturity, while their market price is subject to change with changes in the rate of interest. But because of the early maturity dates of T-bills large interest changes are needed to move T-bills prices very far. Bills are thus regarded as high liquid assets. Commercial paper is a name for short-term unsecured promissory notes issued by corporation. Commercial paper is a means of short-term borrowing by large corporations. Large, well-established corporations have found that borrowing directly from investors through commercial paper is cheaper than relying solely on bank loans. Commercial paper is issued either *directly from the firm to the investor or through an intermediary. Commercial paper, like T-bills is issued at a discount. The most common maturity range of commercial paper is 30 to 60 days or less. Commercial paper is riskier than T-bills, because there is a larger risk that a corporation will default. Also, commercial paper is not easily bought and sold after it is issued, because the issues are relatively small compared with T-bills and hence their market is not liquid. Banker's acceptances are the vehicles created to facilitate commercial trade transactions. These vehicles are called bankers acceptances because a bank accepts the responsibility to repay a loan to the holder of the vehicle in case the debtor fails to perform. Banker's acceptances are short-term fixed-income securities that are created by non-financial firm whose payment is guaranteed by a bank. This short-term loan contract typically has a higher interest rate than similar short –term securities to compensate for the default risk. Since bankers' acceptances are not standardized, there is no active trading of these securities. Repurchase agreement (often referred to as a repo) is the sale of security with a commitment by the seller to buy the security back from the purchaser at a specified price at a designated future date. Basically, a repo is a collectivized short-term loan, where collateral is a security. The collateral in a repo may be a Treasury security, other money-market security. The difference between the purchase price and the sale price is the interest cost of the loan, from which repo rate can be calculated. Because of concern about default risk, the length of maturity of repo is usually very short. If the agreement is for a loan of funds for one day, it is called overnight repo; if the term of the agreement is for more than one day, it is called a term repo. A reverse repo is the opposite of a repo. In this transaction a corporation buys the securities with an agreement to sell them at a specified price and time. Using repos helps to increase the liquidity in the money market. Our focus in this course further will be not investment in short-term vehicles but it is useful for investor to know that short term investment vehicles provide the possibility for temporary investing of money/ funds and investors use these instruments managing their investment portfolio.*

Fixed-income securities are those which return is fixed, up to some redemption date or indefinitely. The fixed amounts may be stated in money terms or indexed to some measure of the price level. This type of financial investments is presented by two different groups of securities: • Long-term debt securities • Preferred stocks. Long-term debt securities can be described as long-term debt instruments representing the issuer's contractual obligation. Long term securities have maturity longer than 1 year. The buyer (investor) of these securities is landing money to the issuer, who undertake obligation periodically to pay interest on this loan and repay the principal at a stated maturity date.

Long-term debt securities are traded in the capital markets. From the investor's point of view these securities can be treated as a "safe" asset. But in reality the safety of investment in fixed –income securities is strongly related with the default risk of an issuer. The major representatives of long-term debt securities are bonds, but today there are a big variety of different kinds of bonds, which differ not only by the different issuers (governments, municipals, companies, agencies, etc.), but by different schemes of interest payments which is a result of bringing financial innovations to the long-term debt securities market. As demand for borrowing the funds from the capital markets is growing the long-term debt securities today are prevailing in the global markets. And it is really become the challenge for investor to pick long-term debt securities relevant to his/ her investment expectations, including the safety of investment. We examine the different kinds of long-term debt securities and their features important to understand for the investor in Chapter 5, together with the other aspects in decision making investing in bonds. Preferred stocks are equity security, which has infinitive life and pay dividends. But preferred stock is attributed to the type of fixed-income securities, because the dividend for preferred stock is fixed in amount and known in advance Though, this security provides for the investor the flow of income very similar to that of the bond. The main difference between preferred stocks and bonds is that for preferred stock the flows are for ever, if the stock is not callable. The preferred stockholders are paid after the debt securities holders but before the common stock holders in terms of priorities in payments of income and in case of liquidation of the company. If the issuer fails to pay the dividend in any year, the unpaid dividends will have to be paid if the issue is cumulative. If preferred stock is issued as noncumulative, dividends for the years with losses do not have to be paid. Usually same rights to vote in general meetings for preferred stockholders are suspended. Because of having the features attributed for both equity and fixed-income securities preferred stocks is known as hybrid security. A most preferred stock is issued as noncumulative and callable. In recent years the preferred stocks with option of convertibility to common stock are proliferating.

The common stock is the other type of investment vehicles which is one of most popular among investors with long-term horizon of their investments. Common stock represents the ownership interest of corporations or the equity of the stock holders. Holders of common stock are entitled to attend and vote at a general meeting of shareholders, to receive declared dividends and to receive their share of the residual assets, if any, if the corporation is bankrupt. The issuers of the common stock are the companies which seek to receive funds in the market and though are "going public". The issuing common stocks and selling them in the market enables the company to raise additional equity capital more easily when using other alternative sources. Thus many companies are issuing their common stocks which are traded in financial markets and investors have wide possibilities for choosing this type of securities for the investment.

Speculative investment vehicles following the term "speculation" could be defined as investments with a high risk and high investment return. Using these investment vehicles speculators try to buy low and to sell high, their primary concern is with anticipating and profiting from the expected market fluctuations. The only gain from such investments is the positive difference between selling and purchasing prices. Of course, using short-term investment strategies investors can use for speculations other investment vehicles, such as common stock, but here we try to accentuate the specific types of investments which are more risky than other investment vehicles because of their nature related with more uncertainty about the changes influencing the their price in the future.

Speculative investment vehicles could be presented by these different vehicles:

- Options;
- Futures;
- Commodities,

traded on the exchange (coffee, grain metals, other commodities);

Options are the derivative financial instruments. An options contract gives the owner of the contract the right, but not the obligation, to buy or to sell a financial asset at a specified price from or to another party. The buyer of the contract must pay a fee (option price) for the seller. There is a big uncertainty about if the buyer of the option will take the advantage of it and what option price would be relevant, as it depends not only on demand and supply in the options market, but on the changes in the other market where the financial asset included in the option contract are traded. Though, the option is a risky financial instrument for those investors who use it for speculations instead of hedging.Futures are the other type of derivatives. A future contract is an agreement between two parties than they agree tom transact with the respect to some financial asset at a predetermined price at a specified future date. One party agree to buy the financial asset, the other agrees to sell the financial asset. It is very important, *that in futures contract case both parties are obligated to perform and neither party charges the fee. There are two types of people who deal with options (and futures) contracts: speculators and hedgers. Speculators buy and sell futures for the sole purpose of making a profit by closing out their positions at a price that is better than the initial price. Such people neither produce nor use the asset in the ordinary course of business. In contrary, hedgers buy and sell futures to offset an otherwise risky position in the market. Transactions using derivatives instruments are not limited to financial assets. There are derivatives, involving different commodities (coffee, grain, precious metals, and other commodities). But in this course the target is on derivatives where underlying asset is a financial asset.*

Other investment tools:

- *Various types of investment funds;*
- *Investment life insurance;*
- *Pension funds;*
- *Hedge funds*

Investment companies/ investment funds. They receive money from investors with the common objective of pooling the funds and then investing them in securities according to a stated set of investment objectives. Two types of funds: • open-end funds (mutual funds) , • closed-end funds (trusts). Open-end funds have no pre-determined amount of stocks outstanding and they can buy back or issue new shares at any point. Price of the share is not determined by demand, but by an estimate of the current market value of the fund's net assets per share (NAV) and a commission. Closed-end funds are publicly traded investment companies that have issued a specified number of shares and can only issue additional shares through a new public issue. Pricing of closed-end funds is different from the pricing of open-end funds: the market price can differ from the NAV. Insurance Companies are in the business of assuming the risks of adverse events (such as fires, accidents, etc.) in exchange for a flow of insurance premiums. Insurance companies are investing the accumulated funds in securities (treasury bonds, corporate stocks and bonds), real estate. Three types of Insurance Companies: life insurance; non-life insurance (also known as property-casualty insurance) and reinsurance. During recent years investment life insurance became very popular investment alternative for individual investors, because this hybrid investment product allows to buy the life insurance policy together with possibility to invest accumulated life insurance payments or lump sum for a long time selecting investment program relevant to investor's future expectations. Pension Funds are an asset pools that accumulates over an employee's working years and pays retirement benefits during the employee's nonworking years. Pension funds are investing the funds according to a stated set of investment objectives in securities (treasury bonds, corporate stocks and bonds), real estate. Hedge funds are unregulated private investment partnerships, limited to institutions and high-net-worth individuals, which seek to exploit various market opportunities and thereby to earn larger returns than are ordinarily available. They require a substantial initial investment from investors and usually have some restrictions on how quickly investor can withdraw their funds. Hedge funds take concentrated speculative positions and can be very risky. It could be noted that originally, the term "hedge" made some sense when applied to these funds. They would by combining different types of investments, including derivatives, try to hedge risk while seeking higher return. But today the word "hedge' is misapplied to these funds because they generally take an aggressive strategies investing in stock, bond and other financial markets around the world and their level of risk is high.

Financial markets

Financial markets are the other important component of investment environment. Financial markets are designed to allow corporations and governments to raise new funds and to allow investors to execute their buying and selling orders. In financial markets funds are channeled from those with the surplus, who buy securities, to those, with shortage, who issue new securities or sell existing securities. A financial market can be seen as a set of arrangements that allows trading among its participants. Financial market provides three important economic functions (Frank J. Fabozzi, 1999): 1. Financial market determines the prices of assets traded through the interactions between buyers and sellers; '

2. Financial market provides a liquidity of the financial assets;

3. Financial market reduces the cost of transactions by reducing explicit costs, such as money spent to advertise the desire to buy or to sell a financial asset. Financial markets could be classified on the bases of those characteristics: • Sequence of transactions for selling and buying securities; • Term of circulation of financial assets traded in the market; • Economic nature of securities, traded in the market; From the perspective of a given country. By sequence of transactions for selling and buying securities:

Primary market

Secondary market

All securities are first traded in the primary market, and the secondary market provides liquidity for these securities. Primary market is where corporate and government entities can raise capital and where the first transactions with the new issued securities are performed. If a company's share is traded in the primary market for the first time this is referred to as an initial public offering (IPO). Investment banks play an important role in the primary market:

• Usually handle issues in the primary market;

• Among other things, act as underwriter of a new issue, guaranteeing the proceeds to the issuer. Secondary market - where previously issued securities are traded among investors. Generally, individual investors do not have access to secondary markets. They use security brokers to act as intermediaries for them. The broker delivers an orders received form investors in securities to a market place, where these orders are executed. Finally, clearing and settlement processes ensure that both sides to these transactions honor their commitment.

Types of brokers:

• Discount broker, who executes only trades in the secondary market;

• Full service broker, who provides a wide range of additional services to clients (ex., advice to buy or sell);

• Online broker is a brokerage firm that allows investors to execute trades electronically using Internet.

Types of secondary market places: • Organized security exchanges; • Over-the-counter markets; • Alternative trading system. An organized security exchange provides the facility for the members to trade securities, and only exchange members may trade there. The members include brokerage firms, which offer their services to individual investors, charging commissions for executing trades on their behalf. Other exchange

By economic nature of securities, traded in the market: Equity market or stock market; Common stock market; Fixed-income market; Debt market; Derivatives market. From the perspective of a given country financial markets are: Internal or national market External or international market.

The internal market can be split into two fractions: domestic market and foreign market. Domestic market is where the securities issued by domestic issuers (companies, Government) are traded. A country's foreign market is where the securities issued by foreign entities are traded. The external market also is called the international market includes the securities which are issued at the same time to the investors in several countries and they are issued outside the jurisdiction of any single country (for example, offshore market). Globalization and integration processes include the integration of financial markets into an international financial market. Because of the globalization of financial markets, potential issuers and investors in any country become not limited to their domestic financial market.

Contents

Foreword

Investment management process Investment management process is the process of managing money or funds. The investment management process describes how an investor should go about making decisions. Investment management process can be disclosed by five-step procedure, which includes following stages: 1. Setting of investment policy. 2. Analysis and evaluation of investment vehicles. 3. Formation of diversified investment portfolio. 4. Portfolio revision 5. Measurement and evaluation of portfolio performance. Setting of investment policy is the first and very important step in investment management process. Investment policy includes setting of investment objectives. The investment policy should have the specific objectives regarding the investment return requirement and risk tolerance of the investor. For example, the investment policy may define that the target of the investment average return should be 15 % and should avoid more than 10 % losses. Identifying investor's tolerance for risk is the most important objective, because it is obvious that every investor would like to earn the highest return possible. But because there is a positive relationship between risk and return, it is not appropriate for an investor to set his/ her investment objectives as just "to make a lot of money". Investment objectives should be stated in terms of both risk and return. The investment policy should also state other important constrains which could influence the investment management. Constrains can include any liquidity needs for the investor, projected investment horizon, as well as other unique needs and preferences of investor. The investment horizon is the period of time for investments. Projected time horizon may be short, long or even indefinite. Setting of investment objectives for individual investors is based on the assessment of their current and future financial objectives. The required rate of return for investment depends on what sum today can be invested and how much investor needs to have at the end of the investment horizon. Wishing to earn higher income on his / her investments investor must assess the level of risk he /she should take and to decide if it is relevant for him or not. The investment policy can include the tax status of the investor. This stage of investment management concludes with the identification of the potential categories of financial assets for inclusion in the investment portfolio. The identification of the potential categories is based on the investment objectives, amount of investable funds, investment horizon and tax status of the investor. we could see that various financial assets by nature may be more or less risky and in general their ability to earn returns differs from one type to the other. As an example, for the investor with low tolerance of risk common stock will be not appropriate type of investment. Analysis and evaluation of investment vehicles. When the investment policy is set up, investor's objectives defined and the potential categories of financial assets for inclusion in the investment portfolio identified, the available investment types can be analyzed. This step involves examining several relevant types of investment vehicles and the individual vehicles inside these groups. For example, if the common stock was identified as investment vehicle relevant for investor, the analysis will be concentrated to the common stock as an investment. The one purpose of such analysis and evaluation is to identify those investment vehicles that currently appear to be mispriced. There are many different approaches how to make such analysis. Most frequently two forms of analysis are used: technical analysis and fundamental analysis. Technical analysis involves the analysis of market prices in an attempt to predict future price movements for the particular financial asset traded on the market.

This analysis examines the trends of historical prices and is based on the assumption that these trends or patterns repeat themselves in the future. Fundamental analysis in its simplest form is focused on the evaluation of intrinsic value of the financial asset. This valuation is based on the assumption that intrinsic value is the present value of future flows from particular investment. By comparison of the intrinsic value and market value of the financial assets those which are under priced or overpriced can be identified. This step involves identifying those specific financial assets in which to invest and determining the proportions of these financial assets in the investment portfolio.

Formation of diversified investment portfolio is the next step in investment management process. Investment portfolio is the set of investment vehicles, formed by the investor seeking to realize its' defined investment objectives. In the stage of portfolio formation the issues of selectivity, timing and diversification need to be addressed by the investor. Selectivity refers to micro forecasting and focuses on forecasting price movements of individual assets. Timing involves macro forecasting of price movements of particular type of financial asset relative to fixed-income securities in general. Diversification involves forming the investor's portfolio for decreasing or limiting risk of investment. 2 techniques of diversification: • random diversification, when several available financial assets are put to the portfolio at random; • objective diversification when financial assets are selected to the portfolio following investment objectives and using appropriate techniques for analysis and evaluation of each financial asset. Investment management theory is focused on issues of objective portfolio diversification and professional investors follow settled investment objectives then constructing and managing their portfolios. Portfolio revision. This step of the investment management process concerns the periodic revision of the three previous stages. This is necessary, because over time investor with long-term investment horizon may change his / her investment objectives and this, in turn means that currently held investor's portfolio may no longer be optimal and even contradict with the new settled investment objectives. Investor should form the new portfolio by selling some assets in his portfolio and buying the others that are not currently held. It could be the other reasons for revising a given portfolio: over time the prices of the assets change, meaning that some assets that were attractive at one time may be no longer be so. Thus investor should sell one asset ant buy the other more attractive in this time according to his/ her evaluation. The decisions to perform changes in revising portfolio depend, upon other things, in the transaction costs incurred in making these changes. For institutional investors portfolio revision is continuing and very important part of their activity. But individual investor managing portfolio must perform portfolio revision periodically as well. Periodic reevaluation of the investment objectives and portfolios based on them is necessary, because financial markets change, tax laws and security regulations change, and other events alter stated investment goals.

Measurement and evaluation of portfolio performance. This the last step in investment management process involves determining periodically how the portfolio performed, in terms of not only the return earned, but also the risk of the portfolio. For evaluation of portfolio performance appropriate measures of return and risk and benchmarks are needed. A benchmark is the performance of predetermined set of assets, obtained for comparison purposes. The benchmark may be a popular index of appropriate assets – stock index, bond index. The benchmarks are widely used by institutional investors evaluating the performance of their portfolios. It is important to point out that investment management process is continuing process influenced by changes in investment environment and changes in investor's attitudes as well. Market globalization offers investors new possibilities, but at the same time investment management become more and more complicated with growing uncertainty.

1. The common target of investment activities is to "employ" the money (funds) during the time period seeking to enhance the investor's wealth. By foregoing consumption today and investing their savings, investors expect to enhance their future consumption possibilities by increasing their wealth. 2. Corporate finance area of studies and practice involves the interaction between firms and financial markets and Investments area of studies and practice involves the interaction between investors and financial markets. Both Corporate Finance and Investments are built upon a common set of financial principles, such as the present value, the future value, the cost of capital). And very often investment and financing analysis for decision making use the same tools, but the interpretation of the results from this analysis for the investor and for the financier would be different. 3. Direct investing is realized using financial markets and indirect investing involves financial intermediaries. The primary difference between these two types of investing is that applying direct investing investors buy and sell financial assets and manage individual investment portfolio themselves; contrary, using indirect type of investing investors are buying or selling financial instruments of financial intermediaries (financial institutions) which invest large pools of funds in the financial markets and hold portfolios. Indirect investing relieves investors from making decisions about their portfolio. 4. Investment environment can be defined as the existing investment vehicles in the market available for investor and the places for transactions with these investment vehicles. 5. The most important characteristics of investment vehicles on which bases the overall variety of investment vehicles can be assorted are the return on investment and the risk which is defined as the uncertainty about the actual return that will be earned on an investment. Each type of investment vehicles could be characterized by certain level of profitability and risk because of the specifics of these financial instruments. The main types of financial investment vehicles are: short- term investment vehicles; fixed-income securities; common stock; speculative investment vehicles; other investment tools. 6. Financial markets are designed to allow corporations and governments to raise new funds and to allow investors to execute their buying and selling orders. In financial markets funds are channeled from those with the surplus, who buy securities, to those, with shortage, who issue new securities or sell existing securities. 7. All securities are first traded in the primary market, and the secondary market provides liquidity for these securities. Primary market is where corporate and government entities can raise capital and where the first transactions with the new issued securities are performed. Secondary market - where previously issued securities are traded among investors. Generally, individual investors do not have access to secondary markets. They use security brokers to act as intermediaries for them. 8. Financial market, in which only short-term financial instruments are traded, is Money market, and financial market in which only long-term financial instruments are traded is Capital market. 9. The investment management process describes how an investor should go about making decisions. Investment management process can be disclosed by five-step procedure, which includes following stages: (1) setting of investment policy; (2) analysis and evaluation of investment vehicles; (3) formation of diversified investment portfolio; (4) portfolio revision; (5) measurement and evaluation of portfolio performance. 10. Investment policy includes setting of investment objectives regarding the investment return requirement and risk tolerance of the investor. The other constrains which investment policy should include and which could influence the investment management are any liquidity needs, projected investment horizon and preferences of the investor. 11. Investment portfolio is the set of investment vehicles, formed by the investor seeking to realize its' defined investment objectives. Selectivity, timing and diversification are the most important issues in the investment portfolio formation. Selectivity refers to micro forecasting and focuses on forecasting price movements of individual assets. Timing involves macro forecasting of price movements of particular type of financial asset relative to fixed-income securities in general. Diversification involves forming the investor's portfolio for decreasing or limiting risk of investment.

CHAPTER ONE

Quantitative methods of investment analysis

1. How to compare different assets in investment selection process? What are the quantitative characteristics of the assets and how to measure them? 2. How does one asset in the same portfolio influence the other one in the same portfolio? And what could be the influence of this relationship to the investor's portfolio? 3. What is relationship between the returns on an asset and returns in the whole market (market portfolio)? The answers of these questions need quantitative methods of analysis, based on the statistical concepts and they will be examined in this chapter. 2.1. Investment income and risk A return is the ultimate objective for any investor. But a relationship between return and risk is a key concept in finance. As finance and investments areas are built upon a common set of financial principles, the main characteristics of any investment are investment return and risk. However to compare various alternatives of investments the precise quantitative measures for both of these characteristics are needed.

Return on investment and expected rate of return General definition of return is the benefit associated with an investment. In most cases the investor can estimate his/ her historical return precisely.

Many investments have two components of their measurable return: a capital gain or loss; some form of income. The rate of return is the percentage increase in returns associated with the holding period: Rate of return = Income + Capital gains / Purchase price (%)

For example, rate of return of the share (r) will be estimated:

$$R = \frac{D + (Pme - Pmb)}{Pmb} \ (\%)$$

Here D - dividends; Pmb - market price of stock at the beginning of holding period; Pme - market price of stock at the end of the holding period. The rate of return, calculated in formulas called holding period return, because its calculation is independent of the passages of the time.

All the investor knows is that there is a beginning of the investment period and an end. The percent calculated using this formula might have been earned over one month or other the year. Investor must be very careful with the interpretation of holding period returns in investment analysis. Investor can't compare the alternative investments using holding period returns, if their holding periods (investment periods) are different. Statistical data which can be used for the investment analysis and portfolio formation deals with a series of holding period returns.

For example, investor knows monthly returns for a year of two stocks. How he/ she can compare these series of returns? In these cases arithmetic average return or sample mean of the returns (ř) can be used:

$$\check{r} = \frac{\sum_{i=1}^{n} r_i}{n},$$

here

ri - rate of return in period i; n - number of observations.

But both holding period returns and sample mean of returns are calculated using historical data. However what happened in the past for the investor is not as important as what happens in the future, because all the investors'decisions are focused to the future, or to expected results from the investments. Of course, no one investor knows the future, but he/ she can use past information and the historical data as well as to use his knowledge and practical experience to make some estimates about it. Analyzing each particular investment vehicle possibilities to earn income in the future investor must think about several „scenarios" of probable changes in macro economy, industry and company which could influence asset prices ant rate of return. Theoretically it could be a series of discrete possible rates of return in the future for the same asset with the different probabilities of earning the particular rate of return. But for the same asset the sum of all probabilities of these rates of returns must be equal to 1 or 100 %. In mathematical statistics it is called simple probability distribution. The expected rate of return E(r) of investment is the statistical measure of return, which is the sum of all possible rates of returns for the same investment weighted by probabilities:

$$E(r) = \sum hi \times ri ,$$
$$i = 1$$

hi - probability of rate of return; ri - rate of return. In all cases than investor has enough information for modeling of future scenarios of changes in rate of return for investment, the decisions should be based on estimated expected rate of return. But sometimes sample mean of return (arithmetic average return) are a useful proxy for the concept of expected rate of return. Sample mean can give an unbiased estimate of the expected value, but obviously it's not perfectly accurate, because based on the assumption that the returns in the future will be the same as in the past. But this is the only one scenario in estimating expected rate of return. It could be expected, that the accuracy of sample mean will increase, as the size of the sample becomes longer (if n will be increased). However, the assumption, that the underlying probability distribution does not change its shape for the longer period becomes more and more unrealistic. In general, the sample mean of returns should be taken for as long time, as investor is confident there has not been significant change in the shape of historical rate of return probability distribution.

Investment risk

Risk can be defined as a chance that the actual outcome from an investment will differ from the expected outcome. Obvious, that most investors are concerned that the actual outcome will be less than the expected outcome. The more variable the possible outcomes that can occur, the greater the risk. Risk is associated with the dispersion in the likely outcome. And dispersion refers to variability. So, the total risk of investments can be measured with such common absolute measures used in statistics as • variance; • standard deviation. Variance can be calculated as a potential deviation of each possible investment rate of return from the expected rate of return: n

$$\delta^2(r) = \sum hi \times [ri - E(r)]^2$$

To compute the variance in formula 2.5 all the rates of returns which were observed in estimating expected rate of return (ri) have to be taken together with their probabilities of appearance (hi). The other an equivalent to variance measure of the total risk is standard deviation which is calculated as the square root of the variance:

$$\delta(r) = \sqrt{\sum hi \times [ri - E(r)]^2}$$

In the cases than the arithmetic average return or sample mean of the returns ($\check{r}$) is used instead of expected rate of return, sample variance ($\delta^2 r$)

can be calculated: n

Σ (rt - ř) ² t=1

δ²r = --------------------

n– 1

Sample standard deviation (δr) consequently can be calculated as the square root of the sample variance: _____ δr = √ δ²r

Variance and the standard deviation are similar measures of risk and can be used for the same purposes in investment analysis; however, standard deviation in practice is used more often. Variance and standard deviation are used when investor is focused on estimating total risk that could be expected in the defined period in the future. Sample variance and sample standard deviation are more often used when investor evaluates total risk of his /her investments during historical period – this is important in investment portfolio management.

Relationship between risk and return The expected rate of return and the variance or standard deviation provide investor with information about the nature of the probability distribution associated with a single asset. However all these numbers are only the characteristics of return and risk of the particular asset. But how does one asset having some specific trade-off between return and risk influence the other one with the different characteristics of return and risk in the same portfolio? And what could be the influence of this relationship to the investor's portfolio? The answers to these questions are of great importance for the investor when forming his/ her diversified portfolio. The statistics that can provide the investor with the information to answer these questions are covariance and correlation coefficient. Covariance and correlation are related and they generally measure the same phenomenon – the relationship between two variables. Both concepts are best understood by looking at the math behind them.

Covariance Two methods of covariance estimation can be used: the sample covariance and the population covariance. The sample covariance is estimated than the investor hasn't enough information about the underlying probability distributions for the returns of two assets and then the sample of historical returns is used. Sample covariance between two assets - A and B is defined in the next formula

Σ [(rA,t - ŕA) × (rB,t - ŕB)] t=1

Cov (ŕA, ŕB) = ---------------------------------------,

n – 1

rA,t , rB,t - consequently, rate of return for assets A and B in the time period t, when t varies from 1 to n; ŕA, ŕB -sample mean of rate of returns for assets A and B consequently. As can be understood from the formula, a number of sample covariance can range from "–" to "+" infinity. Though, the covariance number doesn't tell the investor much about the relationship between the returns on the two assets if only this pair of assets in the portfolio is analysed. It is difficult to conclud if the relationship between returns of two assets (A and B) is strong or weak, taking into account the absolute number of the sample variance. However, what is very important using the covariance for measuring relationship between two assets – the identification of the direction of this relationship. Positive number of covariance shows that rates of return of two assets are moving to the same direction: when return on asset A is above its mean of return (positive), the other asset B is tend to be the same (positive) and vice versa: when the rate of return of asset A is negative or bellow its mean of return, the returns of other asset tend to be negative too. Negative number of covariance shows that rates of return of two assets are moving in the contrariwise directions: when return on asset A is above its mean of return (positive), the returns of the other asset - B is tend to be the negative and vice versa. Though, in analyzing relationship between the assets in the same portfolio using covariance for portfolio formation it is important to identify which of the three possible outcomes exists: positive covariance ("+"), negative covariance ("-") or zero covariance ("0"). If the positive covariance between two assets is identified the common recommendation for the investor would be not to put both of these assets to the same portfolio, because their returns move in the same direction and the risk in portfolio will be not diversified. If the negative covariance between the pair of assets is identified the common recommendation for the investor would be to include both of these assets to the portfolio, because their returns move in the contrariwise directions and the risk in portfolio could be diversified or decreased. If the zero covariance between two assets is identified it means that there is no relationship between the rates of return of two assets. The assets could be included in the same portfolio, but it is rare case in practice and usually covariance tends to be positive or negative. For the investors using the sample covariance as one of the initial steps in analyzing potential assets to put in the portfolio the graphical method instead of analytical one (using formula 2.9) could be a good alternative. In figures 2.1, 2.2 and 2.3 the identification of positive, negative and zero covariances is demonstrated in graphical way. In all these figures the horizontal axis shows the rates of return on asset A and vertical axis shows the rates of return on asset B. When the sample mean of return for both assets is calculated from historical data given, the all area of possible historical rates of return can be divided into four sections (I, II, III and IV) on the basis of the mean returns of two assets (ŕA, ŕB consequently). In I section both asset A and asset B have the positive rates of returns above their means of return; in section II the results are negative for asset A and positive for asset B; in section III the results of both assets are negative – below their meansof return and in section IV the results are positive for asset A and negative for asset B. When the historical rates of return of two assets known for the investor are marked in the area formed by axes ŕA, ŕB, it is very easy to identify what kind of relationship between two assets exists simply by calculating the number of observations in each: if the number of observations in sections I and III prevails over the number of observations in sections II and IV, the covariance between two assets is positive ("+"); if the number of observations in sections II and IV prevails over the number of observations in sections I and III, the covariance between two assets is negative("-"); if the number of observations in sections I and III equals the number of observations in sections II and IV, there is the zero covariance between two assets ("0").

The population covariance is estimated when the investor has enough information about the underlying probability distributions for the returns of two assets and can identify the actual probabilities of various pairs of the returns for two assets at the same time.

The population covariance between stocks A and B: m

Cov (rA, rB) = Σ hi × [rA,i - E(rA)] × [rB,i - E(rB)]

Similar to using the sample covariance, in the population covariance case the graphical method can be used for the identification of the direction of the relationship between two assets. But the graphical presentation of data in this case is more complicated because three dimensions must be used (including the probability). Despite of it, if investor observes that more pairs of returns are in the sections I and III than in II and IV, the population covariance will be positive, if the pairs of return in II and IV prevails over I and III, the population covariance is negative.

. Correlation and Coefficient of determination. Correlation is the degree of relationship between two variables. The correlation coefficient between two assets is closely related to their covariance. The correlation coefficient between two assets A and B (kAB) can be calculated using the next formula:

Cov(rA,rB)

kA,B = ------------------- ,

δ (rA) × δ(rB)

here δ (rA) and δ(rB) are standard deviation for asset A and B consequently. Very important, that instead of covariance when the calculated number is unbounded, the correlation coefficient can range only from -1,0 to +1,0. The more close the absolute meaning of the correlation coefficient to 1,0, the stronger the relationship between the returns of two assets. Two variables are perfectly positively correlated if correlation coefficient is +1,0, that means that the returns of two assets have a perfect positive linear relationship to each other and perfectly negatively correlated if correlation coefficient is -1,0, that means the asset returns have a perfect inverse linear relationship to each other But most often correlation between assets returns is imperfect . When correlation coefficient equals 0, there is no linear relationship between the returns on the two assets . Combining two assets with zero correlation with each other reduces the risk of the portfolio. While a zero correlation between two assets returns is better than positive correlation, it does not provide the risk reduction results of a negative correlation coefficient.

CHAPTER TWO

Introduction to investment

WHAT IS AN INVESTMENT?-

For most of your life, you will be earning and spending money. Rarely, though, will your current money income exactly balance with your consumption desires. Sometimes, you may have more money than you want to spend; at other times, you may want to purchase more than you can afford based on your current income. These imbalances will lead you either to borrow or to save to maximize the long-run benefits from your income. When current income exceeds current consumption desires, people tend to save the excess. They can do any of several things with these savings. One possibility is to put the money under a mattress or bury it in the backyard until some future time when consumption desires exceed current income. When they retrieve their savings from the mattress or backyard, they have the same amount they saved.

Another possibility is that they can give up the immediate possession of these savings for a future larger amount of money that will be available for future consumption. This trade-off of present consumption for a higher level of future consumption is the reason for saving. What you do with the savings to make them increase over time is investment. 1 Those who give up immediate possession of savings (that is, defer consumption) expect to receive in the future a greater amount than they gave up. Conversely, those who consume more than their current income (that is, borrow) must be willing to pay back in the future more than they borrowed. The rate of exchange between future consumption (future dollars) and current consumption (current dollars) is the pure rate of interest. Both people's willingness to pay this difference for borrowed funds and their desire to receive a surplus on their savings (i.e., some rate of return) give rise to an interest rate referred to as the pure time value of money. This interest rate is established in the capital market by a comparison of the supply of excess income available (savings) to be invested and the demand for excess consumption (borrowing) at a given time. If you can exchange $100 of certain income today for $104 of certain income one year from today, then the pure rate of exchange on a risk-free investment (that is, the time value of money) is said to be 4 percent (104/100 – 1). The investor who gives up $100 today expects to consume $104 of goods and services in the future. This assumes that the general price level in the economy stays the same. This price stability has rarely been the case during the past several decades when inflation rates have varied from 1.1 percent in 1986 to as much as 13.3 percent in 1979, with a geometric average of 4.4 percent a year from 1970 to 2010. If investors expect a change in prices, they will require a higher rate of return to compensate for it. For example, if an investor expects a rise in prices (that is, he or she expects inflation) at the annual rate of 2 percent during the period of investment, he or she will increase the required interest rate by 2 percent. In our example, the investor would require $106 in the future to defer the $100 of consumption during an inflationary period (a 6 percent nominal, risk-free interest rate will be required instead of 4 percent). Further, if the future payment from the investment is not certain, the investor will demand an interest rate that exceeds the nominal risk-free interest rate. The uncertainty of the payments from an investment is the investment risk. The additional return added to the nominal, risk-free interest rate is called a risk premium. In our previous example, the investor would require more than $106 one year from today to compensate for the uncertainty. As an example, if the required amount were $110, $4 (4 percent) would be considered a risk premium. 1.1.1 Investment Defined From our discussion, we can specify a formal definition of an investment. Specifically, an investment is the current commitment of dollars for a period of time in order to derive future payments that will compensate the investor for (1) the time the funds are committed, (2) the expected rate of inflation during this time period, and (3) the uncertainty of the future payments. The "investor" can be an individual, a government, a pension fund, or a corporation. Similarly, this definition includes all types of investments, including investments by corporations in plant and equipment and investments by individuals in stocks, bonds, commodities, or real estate. This text emphasizes investments by individual investors. In all cases, the investor is trading a known dollar amount today for some expected future stream of payments that will be greater than the current dollar amount today. At this point, we have answered the questions about why people invest and what they want from their investments. They invest to earn a return from savings due to their deferred consumption. They want a rate of return that compensates them for the time period of the investment, the expected rate of inflation, and the uncertainty of the future cash flows. This return, the investor's required rate of return, is discussed throughout this book. A central question of this book is how investors select investments that will give them their required rates of return.

The next section of this chapter describes how to measure the expected or historical rate of return on an investment and also how to quantify the uncertainty (risk) of expected returns. You need to understand these techniques for measuring the rate of return and the uncertainty of these returns to evaluate the suitability of a particular investment. Although our emphasis will be on financial assets, such as bonds and stocks, we will refer to other assets, such as art and antiques. Chapter 3 discusses the range of financial assets and also considers some nonfinancial assets. 1.2 MEASURES OF RETURN AND RISK The purpose of this book is to help you understand how to choose among alternative investment assets. This selection process requires that you estimate and evaluate the expected riskreturn trade-offs for the alternative investments available. Therefore, you must understand how to measure the rate of return and the risk involved in an investment accurately. To meet this need, in this section we examine ways to quantify return and risk. The presentation will consider how to measure both historical and expected rates of return and risk. We consider historical measures of return and risk because this book and other publications provide numerous examples of historical average rates of return and risk measures for various assets, and understanding these presentations is important. In addition, these historical results are often used by investors when attempting to estimate the expected rates of return and risk for an asset class. The first measure is the historical rate of return on an individual investment over the time period the investment is held (that is, its holding period). Next, we consider how to measure the average historical rate of return for an individual investment over a number of time periods. The third subsection considers the average rate of return for a portfolio of investments. Given the measures of historical rates of return, we will present the traditional measures of risk for a historical time series of returns (that is, the variance and standard deviation). Following the presentation of measures of historical rates of return and risk, we turn to estimating the expected rate of return for an investment. Obviously, such an estimate contains a great deal of uncertainty, and we present measures of this uncertainty or risk. 1.2.1 Measures of Historical Rates of Return When you are evaluating alternative investments for inclusion in your portfolio, you will often be comparing investments with widely different prices or lives. As an example, you might want to compare a $10 stock that pays no dividends to a stock selling for $150 that pays dividends of $5 a year. To properly evaluate these two investments, you must accurately compare their historical rates of returns. A proper measurement of the rates of return is the purpose of this section. When we invest, we defer current consumption in order to add to our wealth so that we can consume more in the future. Therefore, when we talk about a return on an investment, we are concerned with the change in wealth resulting from this investment. This change in wealth can be either due to cash inflows, such as interest or dividends, or caused by a change in the price of the asset (positive or negative). If you commit $200 to an investment at the beginning of the year and you get back $220 at the end of the year, what is your return for the period? The period during which you own an investment is called its holding period, and the return for that period is the holding period return (HPR).

1.2.2 Computing Mean Historical Returns Now that we have calculated the HPY for a single investment for a single year, we want to consider mean rates of return for a single investment and for a portfolio of investments. Over a number of years, a single investment will likely give high rates of return during some years and low rates of return, or possibly negative rates of return, during others. Your analysis should consider each of these returns, but you also want a summary figure that indicates this investment's typical experience, or the rate of return you might expect to receive if you owned this investment over an extended period of time. You can derive such a summary figure by computing the mean annual rate of return (its HPY) for this investment over some period of time. Alternatively, you might want to evaluate a portfolio of investments that might include similar investments (for example, all stocks or all bonds) or a combination of investments (for example, stocks, bonds, and real estate). In this instance, you would calculate the mean rate of return for this portfolio of investments for an individual year or for a number of years. Single Investment Given a set of annual rates of return (HPYs) for an individual investment, there are two summary measures of return performance. The first is the arithmetic mean return, the second is the geometric mean return.

Investors are typically concerned with long-term performance when comparing alternative investments. GM is considered a superior measure of the long-term mean rate of return because it indicates the compound annual rate of return based on the ending value of the investment versus its beginning value.3 Specifically, using the prior example, if we compounded 3.353 percent for three years, (1.03353)3 , we would get an ending wealth value of 1.104. Although the arithmetic average provides a good indication of the expected rate of return for an investment during a future individual year, it is biased upward if you are attempting to measure an asset's long-term performance. This is obvious for a volatile security. Consider, for example, a security that increases in price from $50 to $100 during year 1 and drops back to $50 during year 2.

When rates of return are the same for all years, the GM will be equal to the AM. If the rates of return vary over the years, the GM will always be lower than the AM. The difference between the two mean values will depend on the year-to-year changes in the rates of return. Larger annual changes in the rates of return—that is, more volatility—will result in a greater difference between the alternative mean values. We will point out examples of this in subsequent chapters. An awareness of both methods of computing mean rates of return is important because most published accounts of long-run investment performance or descriptions of financial research will use both the AM and the GM as measures of average historical returns. We will also use both throughout this book with the understanding that the AM is best used as an expected value for an individual year, while the GM is the best measure of long-term performance since it measures the compound annual rate of return for the asset being measured. A Portfolio of Investments The mean historical rate of return (HPY) for a portfolio of investments is measured as the weighted average of the HPYs for the individual investments in the portfolio, or the overall percent change in value of the original portfolio. The weights used in computing the averages are the relative beginning market values for each investment; this is referred to as dollar-weighted or value-weighted mean rate of return. This technique is demonstrated by the examples in Exhibit 1.1. As shown, the HPY is the same (9.5 percent) whether you compute the weighted average return using the beginning market value weights or if you compute the overall percent change in the total value of the portfolio. Although the analysis of historical performance is useful, selecting investments for your portfolio requires you to predict the rates of return you expect to prevail. The next section discusses how you would derive such estimates of expected rates of return. We recognize the great uncertainty regarding these future expectations, and we will discuss how one measures this uncertainty, which is referred to as the risk of an investment. 1.2.3 Calculating Expected Rates of Return Risk is the uncertainty that an investment will earn its expected rate of return. In the examples in the prior section, we examined realized historical rates of return. In contrast, an investor who is evaluating a future investment alternative expects or anticipates a certain rate of return. The investor might say that he or she expects the investment will provide a rate of return of 10 percent, but this is actually the investor's most likely estimate, also referred to as a point estimate. Pressed further, the investor would probably acknowledge the uncertainty of this point estimate return and admit the possibility that, under certain conditions, the annual rate of return on this investment might go as low as −10 percent or as high as 25 percent. The point is, the specification of a larger range of possible returns from an investment reflects the investor's uncertainty regarding what the actual return will be. Therefore, a larger range of possible returns implies that the investment is riskier. An investor determines how certain the expected rate of return on an investment is by analyzing estimates of possible returns. To do this, the investor assigns probability values to all possible returns. These probability values range from zero, which means no chance of the return, to one, which indicates complete certainty that the investment will provide the specified rate of return. These probabilities are typically subjective estimates based on the historical performance of the investment or similar investments modified by the investor's expectations for the future. As an example, an investor may know that about 30 percent of the time the rate of return on this particular investment was 10 percent. Using this information along with future expectations regarding the economy, one can derive an estimate of what might happen in the future.

In an alternative scenario, suppose an investor believed an investment could provide several different rates of return depending on different possible economic conditions. As an example, in a strong economic environment with high corporate profits and little or no inflation, the investor might expect the rate of return on common stocks during the next year to reach as high as 20 percent. In contrast, if there is an economic decline with a higher-than-average rate of inflation, the investor might expect the rate of return on common stocks during the next year to be −20 percent. Finally, with no major change in the economic environment, the rate of return during the next year would probably approach the long-run average of 10 percent. The investor might estimate probabilities for each of these economic scenarios based on past experience and the current outlook as follows: Economic Conditions Probability Rate of Return Strong economy, no inflation 0.15 0.20 Weak economy, above-average inflation 0.15 −0.20 No major change in economy 0.70 0.10 This set of potential outcomes can be visualized as shown in Exhibit 1.3. The computation of the expected rate of return [E(Ri)] is as follows: EðRiÞ = ½ð0:15Þð0:20Þ + ½ð0:15Þð− 0:20Þ + ½ð0:70Þð0:10Þ = 0:07 Obviously, the investor is less certain about the expected return from this investment than about the return from the prior investment with its single possible return.

Measuring the Risk of Expected Rates of Return We have shown that we can calculate the expected rate of return and evaluate the uncertainty, or risk, of an investment by identifying the range of possible returns from that investment and assigning each possible return a weight based on the probability that it will occur. Although the graphs help us visualize the dispersion of possible returns, most investors want to quantify this dispersion using statistical techniques. These statistical measures allow you to compare the return and risk measures for alternative investments directly. Two possible measures of risk (uncertainty) have received support in theoretical work on portfolio theory: the variance and the standard deviation of the estimated distribution of expected returns. In this section, we demonstrate how variance and standard deviation measure the dispersion of possible rates of return around the expected rate of return. We will work with the examples discussed earlier.

DETERMINANTS OF REQUIRED RATES OF RETURN In this section, we continue our discussion of factors that you must consider when selecting securities for an investment portfolio. You will recall that this selection process involves finding securities that provide a rate of return that compensates you for: (1) the time value of money during the period of investment, (2) the expected rate of inflation during the period, and (3) the risk involved. The summation of these three components is called the required rate of return. This is the minimum rate of return that you should accept from an investment to compensate you for deferring consumption. Because of the importance of the required rate of return to the total investment selection process, this section contains a discussion of the three components and what influences each of them. The analysis and estimation of the required rate of return are complicated by the behavior of market rates over time. First, a wide range of rates is available for alternative investments at any time. Second, the rates of return on specific assets change dramatically over time. Third, the difference between the rates available (that is, the spread) on different assets changes over time. The yield data in Exhibit 1.5 for alternative bonds demonstrate these three characteristics. First, even though all these securities have promised returns based upon bond contracts, the promised annual yields during any year differ substantially. As an example, during 2009 the average yields on alternative assets ranged from 0.15 percent on T-bills to 7.29 percent for Baa corporate bonds. Second, the changes in yields for a specific asset are shown by the three-month Treasury bill rate that went from 4.48 percent in 2007 to 0.15 percent in 2009. Third, an example of a change in the difference between yields over time (referred to as a spread) is shown by the Baa–Aaa spread.4 The yield spread in 2007 was 91 basis points (6.47–5.56), but the spread in 2009 increased to 198 basis points (7.29–5.31). (A basis point is 0.01 percent.) Because differences in yields result from the riskiness of each investment, you must understand the risk factors that affect the required rates of return and include them in your assessment of investment opportunities. Because the required returns on all investments change over time, and because large differences separate individual investments, you need to be aware of the several components that determine the required rate of return, starting with the risk-free rate. In this chapter we consider the three components of the required rate of return and briefly discuss what affects these components. The presentation in Chapter 11 on valuation theory will discuss the factors that affect these components in greater detail.

1.3.1 The Real Risk-Free Rate The real risk-free rate (RRFR) is the basic interest rate, assuming no inflation and no uncertainty about future flows. An investor in an inflation-free economy who knew with certainty what cash flows he or she would receive at what time would demand the RRFR on an investment. Earlier, we called this the pure time value of money, because the only sacrifice the investor made was deferring the use of the money for a period of time. This RRFR of interest is the price charged for the risk-free exchange between current goods and future goods. Two factors, one subjective and one objective, influence this exchange price. The subjective factor is the time preference of individuals for the consumption of income. When individuals give up $100 of consumption this year, how much consumption do they want a year from now to compensate for that sacrifice? The strength of the human desire for current consumption influences the rate of compensation required. Time preferences vary among individuals, and the market creates a composite rate that includes the preferences of all investors. This composite rate changes gradually over time because it is influenced by all the investors in the economy, whose changes in preferences may offset one another. The objective factor that influences the RRFR is the set of investment opportunities available in the economy. The investment opportunities available are determined in turn by the long-run real growth rate of the economy. A rapidly growing economy produces more and better opportunities to invest funds and experience positive rates of return. A change in the economy's long-run real growth rate causes a change in all investment opportunities and a change in the required rates of return on all investments. Just as investors supplying capital should demand a higher rate of return when growth is higher, those looking to borrow funds to invest should be willing and able to pay a higher rate of return to use the funds for investment because of the higher growth rate and better opportunities. Thus, a positive relationship exists between the real growth rate in the economy and the RRFR. 1.3.2 Factors Influencing the Nominal Risk-Free Rate (NRFR) Earlier, we observed that an investor would be willing to forgo current consumption in order to increase future consumption at a rate of exchange called the risk-free rate of interest. This rate of exchange was measured in real terms because we assume that investors want to increase the consumption of actual goods and services rather than consuming the same amount that had come to cost more money. Therefore, when we discuss rates of interest, we need to differentiate between real rates of interest that adjust for changes in the general price level, as opposed to nominal rates of interest that are stated in money terms. That is, nominal rates of interest that prevail in the market are determined by real rates of interest, plus factors that will affect the nominal rate of interest, such as the expected rate of inflation and the monetary environment. It is important to understand these factors. Notably, the variables that determine the RRFR change only gradually because we are concerned with long-run real growth. Therefore, you might expect the required rate on a risk-free investment to be quite stable over time. As discussed in connection with Exhibit 1.5, rates on three-month T-bills were not stable over the period from 2004 to 2010. This is demonstrated with additional observations in Exhibit 1.6, which contains yields on T-bills for the period 1987–2010. Investors view T-bills as a prime example of a default-free investment because the government has unlimited ability to derive income from taxes or to create money from which to pay interest. Therefore, one could expect that rates on T-bills should change only gradually. In fact, the data in Exhibit 1.6 show a highly erratic pattern. Specifically, there was an increase in yields from 4.64 percent in 1999 to 5.82 percent in 2000 before declining by over 80 percent in three years to 1.01 percent in 2003, followed by an increase to 4.73 percent in 2006, and concluding at 0.14 percent in 2010. Clearly, the nominal rate of interest on a default-free investment is not stable in the long run or the short run, even though the underlying determinants of the RRFR are quite stable. As noted, two other factors influence the nominal risk-free rate (NRFR): (1) the relative ease or tightness in the capital markets, and (2) the expected rate of inflation. Conditions in the Capital Market You will recall from prior courses in economics and finance that the purpose of capital markets is to bring together investors who want to invest savings with companies or governments who need capital to expand or to finance budget deficits. The cost of funds at any time (the interest rate) is the price that equates the current supply and demand for capital. Beyond this long-run equilibrium, change in the relative ease or tightness in the capital market is a short-run phenomenon caused by a temporary disequilibrium in the supply and demand of capital. As an example, disequilibrium could be caused by an unexpected change in monetary policy (for example, a change in the target federal funds rate) or fiscal policy (for example, a change in the federal deficit). Such a change in monetary policy or fiscal policy will produce a change in the NRFR of interest, but the change should be short-lived because, in the longer run, the higher or lower interest rates will affect capital supply and demand. As an example, an increase in the federal deficit caused by an increase in government spending (easy fiscal policy) will increase the demand for capital and increase interest rates. In turn, this increase in interest rates should cause an increase in savings and a decrease in the demand for capital by corporations or individuals. These changes in market conditions should bring rates back to the longrun equilibrium, which is based on the long-run growth rate of the economy.

1.3.3 Risk Premium A risk-free investment was defined as one for which the investor is certain of the amount and timing of the expected returns. The returns from most investments do not fit this pattern. An investor typically is not completely certain of the income to be received or when it will be received. Investments can range in uncertainty from basically risk-free securities, such as T-bills, to highly speculative investments, such as the common stock of small companies engaged in high-risk enterprises. Most investors require higher rates of return on investments if they perceive that there is any uncertainty about the expected rate of return. This increase in the required rate of return over the NRFR is the risk premium (RP). Although the required risk premium represents a composite of all uncertainty, it is possible to consider several fundamental sources of uncertainty. In this section, we identify and discuss briefly the major sources of uncertainty, including: (1) business risk, (2) financial risk (leverage), (3) liquidity risk, (4) exchange rate risk, and (5) country (political) risk. Business risk is the uncertainty of income flows caused by the nature of a firm's business. The less certain the income flows of the firm, the less certain the income flows to the investor. Therefore, the investor will demand a risk premium that is based on the uncertainty caused by the basic business of the firm. As an example, a retail food company would typically experience stable sales and earnings growth over time and would have low business risk compared to a firm in the auto or airline industry, where sales and earnings fluctuate substantially over the business cycle, implying high business risk. Financial risk is the uncertainty introduced by the method by which the firm finances its investments. If a firm uses only common stock to finance investments, it incurs only business risk. If a firm borrows money to finance investments, it must pay fixed financing charges (in the form of interest to creditors) prior to providing income to the common stockholders, so the uncertainty of returns to the equity investor increases. This increase in uncertainty because of fixed-cost financing is called financial risk or financial leverage, and it causes an increase in the stock's risk premium. For an extended discussion on this, see Brigham (2010). Liquidity risk is the uncertainty introduced by the secondary market for an investment. When an investor acquires an asset, he or she expects that the investment will mature (as with a bond) or that it will be salable to someone else. In either case, the investor expects to be able to convert the security into cash and use the proceeds for current consumption or other investments. The more difficult it is to make this conversion to cash, the greater the liquidity risk. An investor must consider two questions when assessing the liquidity risk of an investment: How long will it take to convert the investment into cash? How certain is the price to be received? Similar uncertainty faces an investor who wants to acquire an asset: How long will it take to acquire the asset? How uncertain is the price to be paid?5 Uncertainty regarding how fast an investment can be bought or sold, or the existence of uncertainty about its price, increases liquidity risk. A U.S. government Treasury bill has almost no liquidity risk because it can be bought or sold in seconds at a price almost identical to the quoted price. In contrast, examples of illiquid investments include a work of art, an antique, or a parcel of real estate in a remote area. For such investments, it may require a long time to find a buyer and the selling prices could vary substantially from expectations. Investors will increase their required rates of return to compensate for this uncertainty regarding timing and price. Liquidity risk can be a significant consideration when investing in foreign securities depending on the country and the liquidity of its stock and bond markets. Exchange rate risk is the uncertainty of returns to an investor who acquires securities denominated in a currency different from his or her own. The likelihood of incurring this risk is becoming greater as investors buy and sell assets around the world, as opposed to only assets within their own countries. A U.S. investor who buys Japanese stock denominated in yen must consider not only the uncertainty of the return in yen but also any change in the exchange value of the yen relative to the U.S. dollar. That is, in addition to the foreign firm's business and financial risk and the security's liquidity risk, the investor must consider the additional uncertainty of the return on this Japanese stock when it is converted from yen to U.S. dollars. As an example of exchange rate risk, assume that you buy 100 shares of Mitsubishi Electric at 1,050 yen when the exchange rate is 105 yen to the dollar. The dollar cost of this investment would be about $10.00 per share (1,050/105). A year later you sell the 100 shares at 1,200 yen when the exchange rate is 115 yen to the dollar. When you calculate the HPY in yen, you find the stock has increased in value by about 14 percent (1,200/1,050) – 1, but this is the HPY for a Japanese investor. A U.S. investor receives a much lower rate of return, because during this period the yen has weakened relative to the dollar by about 9.5 percent (that is, it requires more yen to buy a dollar—115 versus 105). At the new exchange rate, the stock is worth $10.43 per share (1,200/115). Therefore, the return to you as a U.S. investor would be only about 4 percent ($10.43/$10.00) versus 14 percent for the Japanese investor. The difference in return for the Japanese investor and U.S. investor is caused by exchange rate risk—that is, the decline in the value of the yen relative to the dollar. Clearly, the exchange rate could have gone in the other direction, the dollar weakening against the yen. In this case, as a U.S. investor, you would have experienced the 14 percent return measured in yen, as well as a currency gain from the exchange rate change. The more volatile the exchange rate between two countries, the less certain you would be regarding the exchange rate, the greater the exchange rate risk, and the larger the exchange rate risk premium you would require. For an analysis of pricing this risk, see Jorion (1991). There can also be exchange rate risk for a U.S. firm that is extensively multinational in terms of sales and expenses. In this case, the firm's foreign earnings can be affected by changes in the exchange rate. As will be discussed, this risk can generally be hedged at a cost. Country risk, also called political risk, is the uncertainty of returns caused by the possibility of a major change in the political or economic environment of a country. The United States is acknowledged to have the smallest country risk in the world because its political and economic systems are the most stable. During the spring of 2011, prevailing examples include the deadly rebellion in Libya against Moammar Gadhafi; a major uprising in Syria against President Bashar al-Assad; and significant protests in Yemen against President Ali Abdullah Saleh. In addition, there has been a recent deadly earthquake and tsunami in Japan that is disturbing numerous global corporations and the currency markets. Individuals who invest in countries that have unstable political or economic systems must add a country risk premium when determining their required rates of return. When investing globally (which is emphasized throughout the book, based on a discussion in Chapter 3), investors must consider these additional uncertainties. How liquid are the secondary markets for stocks and bonds in the country? Are any of the country's securities traded on major stock exchanges in the United States, London, Tokyo, or Germany? What will happen to exchange rates during the investment period? What is the probability of a political or economic change that will adversely affect your rate of return? Exchange rate risk and country risk differ among countries. A good measure of exchange rate risk would be the absolute variability of the exchange rate relative to a composite exchange rate. The analysis of country risk is much more subjective and must be based on the history and current political environment of the country. This discussion of risk components can be considered a security's fundamental risk because it deals with the intrinsic factors that should affect a security's volatility of returns over time. In subsequent discussion, the standard deviation of returns for a security is referred to as a measure of the security's total risk, which considers only the individual stock—that is, the stock is not considered as part of a portfolio .

1.3.4 Risk Premium and Portfolio Theory An alternative view of risk has been derived from extensive work in portfolio theory and capital market theory by Markowitz (1952, 1959) and Sharpe (1964). These theories are dealt with in greater detail in Chapter 7 and Chapter 8 but their impact on a stock's risk premium should be mentioned briefly at this point. These prior works by Markowitz and Sharpe indicated that investors should use an external market measure of risk. Under a specified set of assumptions, all rational, profit-maximizing investors want to hold a completely diversified market portfolio of risky assets, and they borrow or lend to arrive at a risk level that is consistent with their risk preferences. Under these conditions, they showed that the relevant risk measure for an individual asset is its comovement with the market portfolio. This comovement, which is measured by an asset's covariance with the market portfolio, is referred to as an asset's systematic risk, the portion of an individual asset's total variance that is attributable to the variability of the total market portfolio. In addition, individual assets have variance that is unrelated to the market portfolio (the asset's nonmarket variance) that is due to the asset's unique features. This nonmarket variance is called unsystematic risk, and it is generally considered unimportant because it is eliminated in a large, diversified portfolio. Therefore, under these assumptions, the risk premium for an individual earning asset is a function of the asset's systematic risk with the aggregate market portfolio of risky assets. The measure of an asset's systematic risk is referred to as its beta: Risk Premium = f (Systematic Market Risk) 1.3.5 Fundamental Risk versus Systematic Risk Some might expect a conflict between the market measure of risk (systematic risk) and the fundamental determinants of risk (business risk, and so on). A number of studies have examined the relationship between the market measure of risk (systematic risk) and accounting variables used to measure the fundamental risk factors, such as business risk, financial risk, and liquidity risk. The authors of these studies (especially Thompson, 1976) have generally concluded that a significant relationship exists between the market measure of risk and the fundamental measures of risk. Therefore, the two measures of risk can be complementary. This consistency seems reasonable because one might expect the market measure of risk to reflect the fundamental risk characteristics of the asset. For example, you might expect a firm that has high business risk and financial risk to have an above-average beta. At the same time, as we discuss in Chapter 8, a firm that has a high level of fundamental risk and a large standard deviation of returns can have a lower level of systematic risk simply because the variability of its earnings and its stock price is not related to the aggregate economy or the aggregate market, i.e., a large component of its total risk is due to unique unsystematic risk. Therefore, one can specify the risk premium for an asset as either: Risk Premium = f (Business Risk, Financial Risk, Liquidity Risk, Exchange Rate Risk, Country Risk) or Risk Premium = f (Systematic Market Risk) 1.3.6 Summary of Required Rate of Return The overall required rate of return on alternative investments is determined by three variables: (1) the economy's RRFR, which is influenced by the investment opportunities in the economy (that is, the long-run real growth rate); (2) variables that influence the NRFR, which include short-run ease or tightness in the capital market and the expected rate of inflation. Notably, these variables, which determine the NRFR, are the same for all investments; and (3) the risk premium on the investment. In turn, this risk premium can be related to fundamental factors, including business risk, financial risk, liquidity risk, exchange rate risk, and country risk, or it can be a function of an asset's systematic market risk (beta).

Measures and Sources of Risk In this chapter, we have examined both measures and sources of risk arising from an investment. The measures of market risk for an investment are: • Variance of rates of return • Standard deviation of rates of return • Coefficient of variation of rates of return (standard deviation/means) • Covariance of returns with the market portfolio (beta) The sources of fundamental risk are: • Business risk • Financial risk • Liquidity risk • Exchange rate risk • Country risk

RELATIONSHIP BETWEEN RISK AND RETURN Previously, we showed how to measure the risk and rates of return for alternative investments and we discussed what determines the rates of return that investors require. This section discusses the risk-return combinations that might be available at a point in time and illustrates the factors that cause changes in these combinations. Exhibit 1.7 graphs the expected relationship between risk and return. It shows that investors increase their required rates of return as perceived risk (uncertainty) increases. The line that reflects the combination of risk and return available on alternative investments is referred to as the security market line (SML). The SML reflects the risk-return combinations available for all risky assets in the capital market at a given time. Investors would select investments that are consistent with their risk preferences; some would consider only low-risk investments, whereas others welcome high-risk investments.

Beginning with an initial SML, three changes in the SML can occur. First, individual investments can change positions on the SML because of changes in the perceived risk of the investments. Second, the slope of the SML can change because of a change in the attitudes of investors toward risk; that is, investors can change the returns they require per unit of risk. Third, the SML can experience a parallel shift due to a change in the RRFR or the expected rate of inflation—i.e., anything that can change in the NRFR. These three possibilities are discussed in this section. 1.4.1 Movements along the SML Investors place alternative investments somewhere along the SML based on their perceptions of the risk of the investment. Obviously, if an investment's risk changes due to a change in one of its fundamental risk sources (business risk, and such), it will move along the SML. For example, if a firm increases its financial risk by selling a large bond issue that increases its financial leverage, investors will perceive its common stock as riskier and the stock will move up the SML to a higher risk position implying that investors will require a higher rate of return. As the common stock becomes riskier, it changes its position on the SML. Any change in an asset that affects its fundamental risk factors or its market risk (that is, its beta) will cause the asset to move along the SML as shown in Exhibit 1.8. Note that the SML does not change, only the position of specific assets on the SML. 1.4.2 Changes in the Slope of the SML The slope of the SML indicates the return per unit of risk required by all investors. Assuming a straight line, it is possible to select any point on the SML and compute a risk premium (RP) for an asset through the equation: 1.13 RPi = E(Ri) − NRFR where: RPi = risk premium for asset i EðRiÞ = the expected return for asset i NRFR = the nominal return on a risk-free asset If a point on the SML is identified as the portfolio that contains all the risky assets in the market (referred to as the market portfolio), it is possible to compute a market RP as follows: 1.14 RPm = E(Rm) − NRFR where: RPm = the risk premium on the market portfolio EðRmÞ = the expected return on the market portfolio NRFR = the nominal return on a risk-free asset This market RP is not constant because the slope of the SML changes over time. Although we do not understand completely what causes these changes in the slope, we do know that there are changes in the yield differences between assets with different levels of risk even though the inherent risk differences are relatively constant. These differences in yields are referred to as yield spreads, and these yield spreads change over time. As an example, if the yield on a portfolio of Aaa-rated bonds is 7.50 percent and the yield on a portfolio of Baa-rated bonds is 9.00 percent, we would say that the yield spread is 1.50 percent. This 1.50 percent is referred to as a credit risk premium because the Baa-rated bond is considered to have higher credit risk—that is, it has a higher probability of default. This Baa–Aaa yield spread is not constant over time, as shown by the substantial volatility in the yield spreads shown in Exhibit 1.9. Although the underlying business and financial risk characteristics for the portfolio of bonds in the Aaa-rated bond index and the Baa-rated bond index would probably not change dramatically over time, it is clear from the time-series plot in Exhibit 1.9 that the difference in yields (i.e., the yield spread) has experienced changes of more than 100 basis points (1 percent) in a short period of time (for example, see the yield spread increases in 1974–1975, 1981–1983, 2001–2002, 2008–2009, and the dramatic declines in yield spread during 1975, 1983–1984, 2003–2004, and the second half of 2009). Such a significant change in the yield spread during a period where there is no major change in the fundamental risk characteristics of Baa bonds relative to Aaa bonds would imply a change in the market RP. Specifically, although the intrinsic financial risk characteristics of the bonds remain relatively constant, investors changed the yield spreads (i.e., the credit risk premiums) they demand to accept this difference in financial risk. This change in the RP implies a change in the slope of the SML. Such a change is shown in Exhibit 1.10. The exhibit assumes an increase in the market risk premium, which means an increase in the slope of the market line. Such a change in the slope of the SML (the market risk premium) will affect the required rate of return for all risky assets. Irrespective of where an investment is on the original SML, its required rate of return will increase, although its intrinsic risk characteristics remain unchanged.

1.4.3 Changes in Capital Market Conditions or Expected Inflation The graph in Exhibit 1.11 shows what happens to the SML when there are changes in one of the following factors: (1) expected real growth in the economy, (2) capital market conditions, or (3) the expected rate of inflation. For example, an increase in expected real growth, temporary tightness in the capital market, or an increase in the expected rate of inflation will cause the SML to experience a parallel shift upward as shown in Exhibit 1.11. The parallel shift occurs because changes in expected real growth or changes in capital market conditions or a change in the expected rate of inflation affect the economy's nominal risk-free rate (NRFR) that impacts all investments, irrespective of their risk levels. 1.4.4 Summary of

Changes in the Required Rate of Return The relationship between risk and the required rate of return for an investment can change in three ways: 1. A movement along the SML demonstrates a change in the risk characteristics of a specific investment, such as a change in its business risk, its financial risk, or its systematic risk (its beta). This change affects only the individual investment.

CHAPTER THREE

The Asset Allocation Decision

The previous chapter informed us that risk drives return. Therefore, the practice of investing funds and managing portfolios should focus primarily on managing risk rather than on managing returns. This chapter examines some of the practical implications of risk management in the context of asset allocation. Asset allocation is the process of deciding how to distribute an investor's wealth among different countries and asset classes for investment purposes. An asset class is comprised of securities that have similar characteristics, attributes, and risk/return relationships. A broad asset class, such as "bonds," can be divided into smaller asset classes, such as Treasury bonds, corporate bonds, and high-yield bonds. We will see that, in the long run, the highest compounded returns will most likely accrue to those investors with larger exposures to risky assets. We will also see that although there are no shortcuts or guarantees to investment success, maintaining a reasonable and disciplined approach to investing will increase the likelihood of investment success over time. The asset allocation decision is not an isolated choice; rather, it is a component of a structured four-step portfolio management process that we present in this chapter. As we will see, the first step in the process is to develop an investment policy statement, or plan, that will guide all future decisions. Much of an asset allocation strategy depends on the investor's policy statement, which includes the investor's goals or objectives, constraints, and investment guidelines. What we mean by an "investor" can range from an individual account to trustees overseeing a corporation's multibillion-dollar pension fund, a university endowment, or an insurance company portfolio. Regardless of who the investor is or how simple or complex the investment needs, he or she should develop a policy statement before making long-term investment decisions. Although most of our examples will be in the context of an individual investor, the concepts we introduce here—investment objectives, constraints, benchmarks, and so on—apply to any investor, individual or institution. We'll review historical data to show the importance of the asset allocation decision and discuss the need for investor education, an important issue for companies who offer retirement or savings plans to their employees. The chapter concludes by examining asset allocation strategies across national borders to show the effect of regulations, market environment, and culture on investing patterns; what is appropriate for a U.S.-based investor is not necessarily appropriate for a non-U.S.-based investor. 2.1 INDIVIDUAL INVESTOR LIFE CYCLE Financial plans and investment needs are as different as each individual. Investment needs change over a person's life cycle. How individuals structure their financial plan should be related to their age, financial status, future plans, risk aversion characteristics, and needs. 2.1.1 The Preliminaries Before embarking on an investment program, we need to make sure other needs are satisfied. No serious investment plan should be started until a potential investor has adequate income to cover living expenses and has a safety net should the unexpected occur. Insurance Life insurance should be a component of any financial plan. Life insurance protects loved ones against financial hardship should death occur before our financial goals are met. The death benefit paid by the insurance company can help pay medical bills and funeral expenses and provide cash that family members can use to maintain their lifestyle, retire debt, or invest for future needs (for example, children's education, spouse retirement). Therefore, one of the first steps in developing a financial plan is to purchase adequate life insurance coverage. Insurance can also serve more immediate purposes, including being a means to meet longterm goals, such as retirement planning. On reaching retirement age, you can receive the cash or surrender value of your life insurance policy and use the proceeds to supplement your retirement lifestyle or for estate planning purposes. Insurance coverage also provides protection against other uncertainties. Health insurance helps to pay medical bills. Disability insurance provides continuing income should you become unable to work. Automobile and home (or rental) insurance provides protection against accidents and damage to cars or residences. Although nobody ever expects to use his or her insurance coverage, a first step in a sound financial plan is to have adequate coverage "just in case." Lack of insurance coverage can ruin the best-planned investment program. Cash Reserve Emergencies, job layoffs, and unforeseen expenses happen, and good investment opportunities emerge. It is important to have a cash reserve to help meet these occasions. In addition to providing a safety cushion, a cash reserve reduces the likelihood of being forced to sell investments at inopportune times to cover unexpected expenses. Most experts recommend a cash reserve equal to about six months' living expenses. Calling it a "cash" reserve does not mean the funds should be in cash; rather, the funds should be in investments you can easily convert to cash with little chance of a loss in value. Money market or short-term bond mutual funds and bank accounts are appropriate vehicles for the cash reserve. Similar to the financial plan, an investor's insurance and cash reserve needs will change over his or her life. The need for disability insurance declines when a person retires. In contrast, other insurance, such as supplemental Medicare coverage or long-term-care insurance, may become more important. 34 Part 1: The Investment Background WWW.YAZDANPRESS.COM 2.1.2 Investment Strategies over an Investor's Lifetime Assuming the basic insurance and cash reserve needs are met, individuals can start a serious investment program with their savings. Because of changes in their net worth and risk tolerance, individuals' investment strategies will change over their lifetime. In the following sections, we review various phases in the investment life cycle. Although each individual's needs and preferences are different, some general traits affect most investors over the life cycle. The four life-cycle phases are shown in Exhibit 2.1 (the third and fourth phases—spending and gifting—are shown as concurrent) and described here. Accumulation Phase Individuals in the early-to-middle years of their working careers are in the accumulation phase. As the name implies, these individuals are attempting to accumulate assets to satisfy fairly immediate needs (for example, a down payment for a house) or longerterm goals (children's college education, retirement). Typically, their net worth is small, and debt from car loans or their own past college loans may be heavy. As a result of their typically long investment time horizon and their future earning ability, individuals in the accumulation phase are willing to make relatively high-risk investments in the hopes of making above-average nominal returns over time. Here we emphasize the wisdom of investing early and regularly in one's life. Funds invested in early life cycle phases, with returns compounding over time, will reap significant financial benefits during later phases. Exhibit 2.2 shows growth from an initial $10,000 investment over 20, 30, and 40 years at assumed annual returns of 7 and 8 percent. The middle-aged person who invests $10,000 "when he or she can afford it" will only reap the benefits of compounding for 20 years or so before retirement. In contrast, a person who begins saving at a younger age will reap the much higher benefits of funds invested for 30 or 40 years. Regularly investing as little as $2,000 a year reaps large benefits over time, as well. As shown in Exhibit 2.2, a person who has invested a total of $90,000—an initial $10,000 investment followed by $2,000 annual investments over 40 years—will have over half a million dollars accumulated assuming the 7 percent return. If the funds are invested more aggressively and earn the 8 percent return, the accumulation will be nearly three-quarters of a million dollars.

Consolidation Phase Individuals in the consolidation phase are typically past the midpoint of their careers, have paid off much or all of their outstanding debts, and perhaps have paid, or have the assets to pay, their children's college bills. Earnings exceed expenses, so the excess can be invested to provide for future retirement or estate planning needs. The typical investment horizon for this phase is still long (20 to 30 years), so moderately high risk investments are attractive. At the same time, because individuals in this phase are concerned about capital preservation, they do not want to take abnormally high risks that may put their current nest egg in jeopardy. Spending Phase The spending phase typically begins when individuals retire. Living expenses are covered by social security income and income from prior investments, including employer pension plans. Because their earning years have concluded (although some retirees take part-time positions or do consulting work), they are very conscious of protecting their capital. At the same time, they must balance their desire to preserve the nominal value of their savings with the need to protect themselves against a decline in the real value of their savings due to inflation. The average 65-year-old person in the United States has a life expectancy of about 20 years. Thus, although their overall portfolio may be less risky than in the consolidation phase, they still need some risky growth investments, such as common stocks, for inflation (purchasing power) protection. The transition into the spending phase requires a sometimes difficult change in mindset; throughout our working life we are trying to save; suddenly we can spend. We tend to think that if we spend less, say 4 percent of our accumulated funds annually instead of 5, 6, or 7 percent, our wealth will last far longer. Although this is correct, a bear market early in our retirement can greatly reduce our accumulated funds. Fortunately, there are planning tools that can give a realistic view of what can happen to our retirement funds should markets fall early in our retirement years;

this insight can assist in budgeting and planning to minimize the chance of spending (or losing) all the saved retirement funds. Annuities, which transfer risk from the individual to the annuity firm (most likely an insurance company), are another possibility. With an annuity, the recipient receives a guaranteed, lifelong stream of income. Options can allow for the annuity to continue until both a husband and wife die. Gifting Phase The gifting phase is similar to, and may be concurrent with, the spending phase. In this stage, individuals may believe they have sufficient income and assets to cover their current and future expenses while maintaining a reserve for uncertainties. In such a case, excess assets can be used to provide financial assistance to relatives or friends, to establish charitable trusts, or to fund trusts as an estate planning tool to minimize estate taxes. Exhibit 2.2 Benefits of Investing Early The Future Value of an Initial $10,000 Investment The Future Value of Investing $2,000 Annually The Future Value of the Initial Investment Plus the Annual Investment Interest rate 7.0% 20 years $38,696.84 $81,990.98 $120,687.83 30 years $76,122.55 $188,921.57 $265,044.12 40 years $149,744.58 $399,270.22 $549,014.80 Interest rate 8.0% 20 years $46,609.57 $91,523.93 $138,133.50 30 years $100,626.57 $226,566.42 $327,192.99 40 years $217,245.21 $518,113.04 $735,358.25 Source: Calculations by authors. 36 Part 1: The Investment Background WWW.YAZDANPRESS.COM 2.1.3 Life Cycle Investment Goals During an individual's investment life cycle, he or she will have a variety of financial goals. Near-term, high-priority goals are shorter-term financial objectives that individuals set to fund purchases that are personally important to them, such as accumulating funds to make a house down payment, buy a new car, or take a trip. Parents with teenage children may have a near-term, high-priority goal to accumulate funds to help pay college expenses. Because of the emotional importance of these goals and their short time horizon, high-risk investments are not usually considered suitable for achieving them. Long-term, high-priority goals typically include some form of financial independence, such as the ability to retire at a certain age. Because of their long-term nature, higher-risk investments can be used to help meet these objectives. Lower-priority goals are just that—it might be nice to meet these objectives, but it is not critical. Examples include the ability to purchase a new car every few years, redecorate the home with expensive furnishings, or take a long, luxurious vacation. A well-developed policy statement considers these diverse goals over an investor's lifetime. The following sections detail the process for constructing an investment policy, creating a portfolio that is consistent with the policy and the environment, managing the portfolio, and monitoring its performance relative to its goals and objectives over time. 2.2 THE PORTFOLIO MANAGEMENT PROCESS* The process of managing an investment portfolio never stops. Once the funds are initially invested according to the plan, the real work begins in evaluating the portfolio's performance and updating the portfolio based on changes in the economic environment and the investor's needs. The first step in the portfolio management process, as seen in Exhibit 2.3, is for the investor, either alone or with the assistance of an investment advisor, to construct a policy statement. The policy statement is a road map; in it, investors specify the types of risks they are willing to take and their investment goals and constraints. All investment decisions are based on the policy statement to ensure that these decisions are appropriate for the investor. We examine the process of constructing a policy statement in the following section. Because investor needs, goals, and constraints change over time, the policy statement must be periodically reviewed and updated. The process of investing involves assessing the future and deriving strategies that offer the best possibility of meeting the policy statement guidelines. In the second step of the portfolio management process, the portfolio manager studies current financial and economic conditions and forecasts future trends. The investor's needs, as reflected in the policy statement, and financial market expectations will jointly determine investment strategy. Economies are dynamic; they are affected by numerous industry struggles, politics, and changing demographics and social attitudes. Thus, the portfolio will require constant monitoring and updating to reflect changes in financial market expectations. We examine the process of evaluating and forecasting economic trends in Chapter 12. The third step of the portfolio management process is to construct the portfolio. With the investor's policy statement and financial market forecasts as input, the advisors implement the investment strategy and determine how to allocate available funds across different countries, asset classes, and securities. This involves constructing a portfolio that will minimize the investor's risks while meeting the needs specified in the policy statement. Financial theory frequently assists portfolio construction, which is discussed in Part 2 of this book. Some of the practical aspects of selecting investments for inclusion in a portfolio are discussed in Part 4 and Part 5. The fourth step in the portfolio management process is the continual monitoring of the investor's needs and capital market conditions and, when necessary, updating the policy statement. Based upon all of this, the investment strategy is modified accordingly. An important component of the monitoring process is to evaluate a portfolio's performance and compare the relative results to the expectations and the requirements listed in the policy statement. The evaluation of portfolio performance is discussed in Chapter 25. Once you have completed the four steps, it is important to recognize that this is a continuous process—it is essential to revisit all the steps to ensure that the policy statement is still valid, that the economic outlook has not changed, and so forth. 2.3 THE NEED FOR A POLICY STATEMENT As noted in the previous section, a policy statement is a road map that guides the investment process. Constructing a policy statement is an invaluable planning tool that will help the investor understand his or her needs better as well as assist an advisor or portfolio manager in managing a client's funds. While it does not guarantee investment success, a policy statement will provide discipline for the investment process and reduce the possibility of making hasty, inappropriate decisions. There are two important reasons for constructing a policy statement: First, it helps the investor decide on realistic investment goals after learning about the financial markets and the risks of investing; second, it creates a standard by which to judge the performance of the portfolio manager. 2.3.1 Understand and Articulate Realistic Investor Goals When asked about their investment goal, people often say, "to make a lot of money," or some similar response. Such a goal has two drawbacks: First, it may not be appropriate for the investor, and second, it is too open-ended to provide guidance for specific investments and time frames. Such an objective is well suited for someone going to the racetrack or buying lottery tickets, but it is inappropriate for someone investing funds in financial and real assets for the long term. An important purpose of writing a policy statement is to help investors understand their own needs, objectives, and investment constraints. As part of this, investors need to learn about financial markets and the risks of investing. This background will help prevent them from making inappropriate investment decisions in the future based on unrealistic expectations and increase the possibility that they will satisfy their specific, measurable financial goals. Thus, the policy statement helps the investor to specify realistic goals and become more informed about the risks and costs of investing. Market values of assets, whether they be stocks, bonds, or real estate, can fluctuate dramatically. For example, during the October 1987 crash, the Dow Jones Industrial Average (DJIA) fell more than 20 percent in one day; in October 1997, the Dow fell "only" 7 percent. A review of market history shows that it is not unusual for asset prices to decline by 10 percent to 20 percent over several months—for example, the months following the market peak in March 2000, and the major decline when the market reopened after September 11, 2001. The most recent "bloodbath" was the market decline of over 30 percent during 2008—and this decline was global. The problem is, investors typically focus on a single statistic, such as an 11 percent average annual rate of return on stocks, and expect the market to rise 11 percent every year. Such thinking ignores the risk of stock investing. Part of the process of developing a policy statement is for the investor to become familiar with the risks of investing, because we know that a strong positive relationship exists between risk and return. In summary, constructing a policy statement is mainly the investor's responsibility. It is a process whereby investors articulate their realistic needs and goals and become familiar with financial markets and investing risks. Without this information, investors cannot adequately communicate their needs to the portfolio manager. Without this input from investors, the portfolio manager cannot construct a portfolio that will satisfy clients' needs. The result of bypassing this step will most likely be future aggravation, dissatisfaction, and disappointment. 2.3.2 Standards for Evaluating Portfolio Performance The policy statement also assists in judging the performance of the portfolio manager. Performance cannot be judged without an objective standard; the policy statement provides that objective standard. The portfolio's performance should be compared to guidelines specified in the policy statement, not on the portfolio's overall return. For example, if an investor has a low tolerance for risky investments, the portfolio manager should not be fired simply because the portfolio does not perform as well as the risky S&P 500 stock index. The point is, because risk drives returns, the investor's lower-risk investments, as specified in the investor's policy statement, will probably earn lower returns than if all the investor's funds were placed in the aggregate stock market. The policy statement will typically include a benchmark portfolio, or comparison standard. The risk of the benchmark, and the assets included in the benchmark, should agree with the client's risk preferences and investment needs. Notably, both the client and the portfolio manager must agree that the benchmark portfolio reflects the risk preferences and appropriate return requirements of the client. In turn, the investment performance of the portfolio manager should be compared to this benchmark portfolio. For example, an investor who specifies lowrisk investments in the policy statement should compare the portfolio manager's performance against a low-risk benchmark portfolio. Likewise, an investor seeking high-risk, high-return investments should compare the portfolio's performance against a high-risk benchmark portfolio. Because it sets an objective performance standard, the policy statement acts as a starting point for periodic portfolio review and client communication with managers. Questions concerning portfolio performance should be addressed in the context of the written policy guidelines. Managers should mainly be judged by whether they consistently followed the client's policy guidelines. The portfolio manager who makes unilateral deviations from policy is not working in the best interests of the client. Therefore, even significant deviations that result in higher portfolio returns can and should be grounds for the manager's dismissal. Thus, we see the importance of constructing the policy statement: The client must first understand his or her own needs before communicating them to the portfolio manager who in turn, must implement the client's desires by following the investment guidelines. As long as policy is followed, shortfalls in performance should not be a major concern. Remember that the policy statement is designed to impose an investment discipline on the client and on the portfolio manager. The less knowledgeable they are, the more likely clients are to inappropriately judge the performance of the portfolio manager. 2.3.3 Other Benefits A sound policy statement helps to protect the client against a portfolio manager's inappropriate investments or unethical behavior. Without clear, written guidance, some managers may consider investing in high-risk investments, hoping to earn a quick return. Such actions are probably counter to the investor's specified needs and risk preferences. Though legal recourse is a possibility against such action, writing a clear and unambiguous policy statement should reduce the possibility of such inappropriate manager behavior. Just because a specific manager currently manages your account does not mean that person will always manage your funds. Because your portfolio manager may be promoted' dismissed or take a better job' your funds may come under the management of an individual you do not know and who does not know you. To prevent costly delays during this transition, you can ensure that the new manager "hits the ground running" with a clearly written policy statement. A policy statement should prevent delays in monitoring and rebalancing your portfolio and contribute to a seamless transition from one money manager to another. To sum up, a clearly written policy statement helps avoid potential problems. When the client clearly specifies his or her needs and desires, the portfolio manager can more effectively construct an appropriate portfolio. The policy statement provides an objective measure for evaluating portfolio performance, helps guard against ethical lapses by the portfolio manager, and aids in the transition between money managers. Therefore, the first step before beginning any investment program is to construct a policy statement.

An appropriate policy statement should satisfactorily answer the following questions: 1. Is the policy carefully designed to meet the specific needs and objectives of this particular investor? (Cookie-cutter or one-size-fits-all policy statements are generally inappropriate.) 2. Is the policy written so clearly and explicitly that a competent stranger could use it to manage the portfolio in conformance with the client's needs? In case of a manager transition, could the new manager use this policy statement to handle your portfolio in accordance with your needs? 3. Would the client have been able to remain committed to the policies during the capital market experiences of the past 60 to 70 years? That is, does the client fully understand investment risks and the need for a disciplined approach to the investment process? 4. Would the portfolio manager have been able to maintain the policies specified over the same period? (Discipline is a two-way street; we do not want the portfolio manager to change strategies because of a disappointing market.) 5. Would the policy, if implemented, have achieved the client's objectives? (Bottom line: Would the policy have worked to meet the client's needs?)

2.4 INPUT TO THE POLICY STATEMENT Before an investor and advisor can construct a policy statement, they need to have an open and frank exchange of information, ideas, fears, and goals. Specifically, the client and advisor need to discuss the client's investment objectives and constraints. To illustrate this framework, we discuss the investment objectives and constraints that may confront "typical" 25-year-old and 65-year-old investors. 2.4.1 Investment Objectives The investor's objectives are his or her investment goals expressed in terms of both risk and returns. The relationship between risk and returns requires that goals not be expressed only in terms of returns. Expressing goals only in terms of returns can lead to inappropriate investment practices by the portfolio manager, such as the use of high-risk investment strategies or account "churning," which involves moving quickly in and out of investments in an attempt to buy low and sell high. For example, a person may have a stated return goal such as "double my investment in five years." Before such a statement becomes part of the policy statement, the client must become fully informed of investment risks associated with such a goal, including the possibility of loss. A careful analysis of the client's risk tolerance should precede any discussion of return objectives. It makes little sense for a person who is risk averse to have his/her funds invested in high-risk assets. Investment firms survey clients to gauge their risk tolerance. Sometimes investment magazines or books contain tests that individuals can take to help them evaluate their risk tolerance (see Exhibit 2.4). Subsequently, an advisor will use the results of this evaluation to categorize a client's risk tolerance and suggest an initial asset allocation such as those contained in Exhibit 2.5. Risk tolerance is more than a function of an individual's psychological makeup; it is affected by other factors, including a person's current insurance coverage and cash reserves. Risk tolerance is also affected by an individual's family situation (for example, marital status and the number and ages of children) and by his or her age. We know that older persons generally have shorter investment time frames within which to make up any losses; they also have years of experience, including living through various market gyrations and "corrections" (a euphemism for downtrends or crashes) that younger people have not experienced or whose effect they do not fully appreciate. Risk tolerance is also influenced by one's current net worth and income expectations. All else being equal, individuals with higher incomes have a greater propensity to undertake risk because their incomes can help cover any shortfall. Likewise, individuals with larger portfolios can afford to place some assets in risky investments while the remaining assets provide a cushion against losses. A person's return objective may be stated in terms of an absolute or a relative percentage return, but it may also be stated in terms of a general goal, such as capital preservation, current income, capital appreciation, or total return. Capital preservation means that investors want to minimize their risk of loss, usually in real terms: They seek to maintain the purchasing power of their investment. In other words, the return needs to be no less than the rate of inflation. Generally, this is a strategy for strongly risk-averse investors or for funds needed in the short run, such as for next year's tuition payment or a down payment on a house. Capital appreciation is an appropriate objective when the investors want the portfolio to grow in real terms over time to meet some future need. Under this strategy, growth mainly occurs through capital gains. This is an aggressive strategy for investors willing to take on risk to meet their objective. Generally, longer-term investors seeking to build a retirement or college education fund may have this goal. When current income is the return objective, the investors want the portfolio to concentrate on generating income rather than capital gains. This strategy sometimes suits investors who want to supplement their earnings with income generated by their portfolio to meet their living expenses. Retirees may favor this objective for part of their portfolio to help generate spendable funds. The objective for the total return strategy is similar to that of capital appreciation; namely, the investors want the portfolio to grow over time to meet a future need. Whereas the capital appreciation strategy seeks to do this primarily through capital gains, the total return strategy seeks to increase portfolio value by both capital gains and reinvesting current income. Because the total return strategy has both income and capital gains components, its risk exposure lies between that of the current income and capital appreciation strategies. Investment Objective: 25-Year-Old What is an appropriate investment objective for our typical 25-year-old investor? Assume he holds a steady job, is a valued employee, has adequate insurance coverage, and has enough money in the bank to provide a cash reserve. Let's also assume that his current long-term, high-priority investment goal is to build a retirement fund. Depending on his risk preferences, he can select a strategy carrying moderate to high amounts of risk because the income stream from his job will probably grow over time. Further, given his young age and income growth potential, a low-risk strategy, such as capital preservation or current income, is inappropriate for his retirement fund goal; a total return or capital appreciation objective would be most appropriate. Here's a possible objective statement: Invest funds in a variety of moderate- to higher-risk investments. The average risk of the equity portfolio should exceed that of a broad stock market index, such as the NYSE stock index. Foreign and domestic equity exposure should range from 80 percent to 95 percent of the total portfolio. Remaining funds should be invested in short- and intermediate-term notes and bonds. Investment Objective: 65-Year-Old Assume our typical 65-year-old investor likewise has adequate insurance coverage and a cash reserve. Let's also assume she is retiring this year. This individual will want less risk exposure than the 25-year-old investor because her earning power from employment will soon be ending; she will not be able to recover any investment losses by saving more out of her paycheck. Depending on her income from social security and a pension plan, she may need some current income from her retirement portfolio to meet living expenses. Given that she can be expected to live an average of another 20 years, she will need protection against inflation. A risk-averse investor will choose a combination of current income and capital preservation strategy; a more risk-tolerant investor will choose a combination of current income and total return in an attempt to have principal growth outpace inflation. Here's an example of such an objective statement: Invest in stock and bond investments to meet income needs (from bond income and stock dividends) and to provide for real growth (from equities). Fixed-income securities should comprise 55–65 percent of the total portfolio; of this, 5–15 percent should be invested in short-term securities for extra liquidity and safety. The remaining 35–45 percent of the portfolio should be invested in high-quality stocks whose risk is similar to the S&P 500 index. More detailed analyses for our 25-year-old and our 65-year-old would make more specific assumptions about the risk tolerance of each, as well as clearly enumerate their investment goals, return objectives, the funds they have to invest at the present, the funds they expect to invest over time, and the benchmark portfolio that will be used to evaluate performance. 2.4.2 Investment Constraints In addition to the investment objective that sets limits on risk and return, certain other constraints also affect the investment plan. Investment constraints include liquidity needs, an investment time horizon, tax factors, legal and regulatory constraints, and unique needs and preferences. Liquidity Needs An asset is liquid if it can be quickly converted to cash at a price close to fair market value. Generally, assets are more liquid if many traders are interested in a fairly standardized product. Treasury bills are a highly liquid security, and real estate and venture capital are not. Investors may have liquidity needs that the investment plan must consider. For example, although an investor may have a primary long-term goal, several near-term goals may require available funds. Wealthy individuals with sizable tax obligations need adequate liquidity to pay their taxes without upsetting their investment plan. Some retirement plans may need funds for shorter-term purposes, such as buying a car or a house or making college tuition payments. Our typical 25-year-old investor probably has little need for liquidity as he focuses on his long-term retirement fund goal. This constraint may change, however, should he face a period of unemployment or should near-term goals, such as honeymoon expenses or a house down payment, enter the picture. Should any changes occur, the investor needs to revise his policy statement and financial plans accordingly. Our soon-to-beretired 65-year-old investor has a greater need for liquidity. Although she may receive regular checks from her pension plan and social security, it is not likely that they will equal her working paycheck. She will want some of her portfolio in liquid securities to meet unexpected expenses, bills, or special needs such as trips or cruises. Time Horizon Time horizon as an investment constraint briefly entered our earlier discussion of near-term and long-term high-priority goals. A close (but not perfect) relationship exists between an investor's time horizon, liquidity needs, and ability to handle risk. Investors with long investment horizons generally require less liquidity and can tolerate greater portfolio risk: less liquidity because the funds are not usually needed for many years; greater risk tolerance because any shortfalls or losses can be overcome by earnings and returns in subsequent years. Investors with shorter time horizons generally favor more liquid and less risky investments because losses are harder to overcome during a short time frame. Because of life expectancies, our 25-year-old investor has a longer investment time horizon than our 65-year-old investor. But, as discussed earlier, this does not mean the 65-year-old should place all her money in short-term CDs; she needs the inflation protection that long-term investments Chapter 2: The Asset Allocation Decision 45 WWW.YAZDANPRESS.COM such as common stock can provide. Still, because of the time horizon constraint, the 25-year-old can have a greater proportion of his portfolio in equities—including stocks in small firms, as well as international and emerging market firms—than the 65-year-old. Tax Concerns Investment planning is complicated by the tax code; taxes complicate the situation even more if international investments are part of the portfolio. Taxable income from interest, dividends, or rents is taxable at the investor's marginal tax rate. The marginal tax rate is the proportion of the next one dollar in income paid as taxes. Exhibit 2.6 shows the marginal tax rates for different levels of taxable income. As of 2011, the top federal marginal tax rate was 35 percent. Capital gains or losses arise from asset price changes. They are taxed differently than income. Income is taxed when it is received; capital gains or losses are taxed only when an asset is sold and the gain or loss, relative to its initial cost or basis, is realized. Unrealized capital gains (or losses) reflect the price change in currently held assets that have not been sold; the tax liability on unrealized capital gains can be deferred indefinitely. If appreciated assets are passed on to an heir upon the investor's death, the basis of the assets is considered to be their value on the date of the holder's death. The heirs can then sell the assets and pay lower capital gains taxes if they wish. Realized capital gains occur when an appreciated asset is sold; taxes are due on the realized capital gains only. As of 2011, the maximum tax rate on stock dividends and long-term capital gains is 15 percent. Some find the difference between average and marginal income tax rates confusing. The marginal tax rate is the part of each additional dollar in income that is paid as tax. Thus, a married person, filing jointly, with an income of $50,000 will have a marginal tax rate of 15 percent. The 15 percent marginal tax rate should be used to determine after-tax returns on investments. The average tax rate is simply a person's total tax payment divided by their total income. It represents the average tax paid on each dollar the person earned. From Exhibit 2.6, a married person, filing jointly, will pay $6,650 in tax on a $50,000 income [$1,700 + 0.15($50,000 – $17,000)]. This average tax rate is $6,650/$50,000 or 13.3 percent. Note that the average tax rate is a weighted average of the person's marginal tax rates paid on each dollar of income.

The first $17,000 of income has a 10 percent marginal tax rate; the next $33,000 has a 15 percent marginal tax rate: $17,000 $50,000 × 0:10 + $33,000 $50,000 × 0:15 = 0:133, or the average tax rate of 13:3 percent Another tax factor is that some sources of investment income are exempt from federal and state taxes. For example, interest on federal securities, such as Treasury bills, notes, and bonds, is exempt from state taxes. Interest on municipal bonds (bonds issued by a state or other local governing body) is exempt from federal taxes. Further, if investors purchase municipal bonds issued by a local governing body of the state in which they live, the interest may be exempt from both state and federal income tax. Thus, high-income individuals have an incentive to purchase municipal bonds to reduce their tax liabilities. The after-tax return on taxable investment income is After-Tax Income Return = Pre-Tax Income Return × ð1 – Marginal Tax RateÞ Thus, the after-tax return on a taxable bond investment should be compared to that of municipals before deciding which security a tax-paying investor should purchase.1 Alternatively, we could compute a municipal's equivalent taxable yield, which is what a taxable bond investment would have to offer to produce the same after-tax return as the municipal. It is given by Equivalent Taxable Yield = ðMunicipal YieldÞ ð1 – Marginal Tax RateÞ To illustrate, if an investor is in the 28 percent marginal tax bracket, a taxable investment yield of 8 percent has an after-tax yield of 8 percent × (1 – 0.28) or 5.76 percent; an equivalent-risk municipal security offering a yield greater than 5.76 percent offers the investor greater after-tax returns. On the other hand, a municipal bond yielding 6 percent has an equivalent taxable yield of: 6 percent/(1 – 0.28) = 8.33 percent; to earn more money after taxes, an equivalent-risk taxable investment has to offer a return greater than 8.33 percent. There are other means of reducing investment tax liabilities. Contributions to an IRA (individual retirement account) may qualify as a tax deduction if certain income limits are met. Even without that deduction, taxes on any investment returns of an IRA, including any income, are deferred until the funds are withdrawn from the account. Any funds withdrawn from an IRA are taxable as current income, regardless of whether growth in the IRA occurs as a result of capital gains, income, or both. For this reason, to minimize taxes advisors recommend investing in stocks in taxable accounts and in bonds in tax-deferred accounts such as IRAs. When funds are withdrawn from a tax-deferred account such as a regular IRA, assets are taxed (at most) at a 35 percent income tax rate (Exhibit 2.6)—even if the source of the stock return is primarily capital gains. In a taxable account, capital gains are taxed at the maximum 15 percent capital gains rate. Decisions regarding IRAs (including Roth IRAs) are very important, but the details of such decisions are beyond the purpose of this book. Therefore, we recommend that investors discuss these decisions with a tax consultant or financial planner. Legal and Regulatory Factors Both the investment process and the financial markets are highly regulated and subject to numerous laws. At times, these legal and regulatory factors constrain the investment strategies of individuals and institutions. For example, funds removed from a regular IRA, Roth IRA, or 401(k) plan before age 59½ are taxable and subject to an additional 10 percent withdrawal penalty. You may also be familiar with the tag line in many bank CD advertisements—"substantial interest penalty upon early withdrawal." Regulations and rules such as these may make such investments unattractive for investors with substantial liquidity needs in their portfolios. Regulations can also constrain the investment choices available to someone in a fiduciary role. A fiduciary, or trustee, supervises an investment portfolio of a third party, such as a trust account or discretionary account.2 The fiduciary must make investment decisions in accordance with the owner's wishes; a properly written policy statement assists this process. In addition, trustees of a trust account must meet the prudent-man standard, which means that they must invest and manage the funds as a prudent person would manage his or her own affairs. Notably, the prudent-man standard is based on the composition of the entire portfolio, not each individual asset.3 All investors must respect certain laws, such as insider trading prohibitions against the purchase and sale of securities on the basis of important information that is not publicly known. Typically, the people possessing such private, or insider, information are the firm's managers, who have a fiduciary duty to their shareholders. Security transactions based on access to insider information violates the fiduciary trust the shareholders have placed with management because the managers seek personal financial gain from their privileged position as agents for the shareholders. For our typical 25-year-old investor, legal and regulatory matters will be of little concern, with the possible exception of insider trading laws and the penalties associated with early withdrawal of funds from tax-deferred retirement accounts. Should he seek a financial advisor to assist him in constructing a financial plan, that advisor would have to obey the regulations pertinent to a client-advisor relationship. Similar concerns confront our 65-year-old investor. In addition, as a retiree, if she wants to do estate planning and set up trust accounts, she should seek legal and tax advice to ensure that her plans are properly implemented. Unique Needs and Preferences This category covers the individual and sometimes idiosyncratic concerns of each investor. Some investors may want to exclude certain investments from their portfolio solely on the basis of personal preference or for social consciousness reasons. For example, they may request that no firms that manufacture or sell tobacco, alcohol, pornography, or environmentally harmful products be included in their portfolio. Some mutual funds screen according to this type of social responsibility criterion. Another example of a personal constraint is the time and expertise a person has for managing his or her portfolio. Busy executives may prefer to relax during nonworking hours and let a trusted advisor manage their investments. Retirees, on the other hand, may have the time but believe they lack the expertise to choose and monitor investments, so they also may seek professional advice. In addition, a business owner with a large portion of her wealth—and emotion—tied up in her firm's stock may be reluctant to sell even when it may be financially prudent to do so and then reinvest the proceeds for diversification purposes. Further, if the stock holdings are in a private company, it may be difficult to find a buyer unless shares are sold at a discount from their fair market value. Because each investor is unique, the implications of this final constraint differ for each person; there is no "typical" 25-year-old or 65-year-old investor. The point is, each individual will have to decide on—and then communicate—specific needs and preferences in a well-constructed policy statement.

2.5 CONSTRUCTING THE POLICY STATEMENT As we have seen, the policy statement allows the investor to communicate his or her objectives (risk and return) and constraints (liquidity, time horizon, tax, legal and regulatory, and unique needs and preferences). This communication gives the advisor a better chance of implementing an investment strategy that will satisfy the investor. Even if an advisor is not used, each investor needs to take this first important step of the investment process and develop a financial plan to guide the investment strategy. To do without a plan or to plan poorly is to place the success of the financial plan in jeopardy. 2.5.1 General Guidelines Constructing a policy statement is the investor's responsibility, but investment advisors often assist in the process. Here, for both the investor and the advisor, are guidelines for good policy statement construction. In the process of constructing a policy statement, investors should think about the set of questions suggested previously on page 39. When working with an investor to create a policy statement, an advisor should ensure that the policy statement satisfactorily answers the questions suggested previously on page 41. 2.5.2 Some Common Mistakes When constructing their policy statements, participants in employer-sponsored retirement plans need to realize that in many such plans 30–40 percent of their retirement funds may be invested in their employer's stock. Having so much money invested in one asset violates diversification principles and could be costly. To put this in context, most mutual funds are limited by law to having no more than 5 percent of their assets in any one company's stock; a firm's pension plan can invest no more than 10 percent of their funds in its own stock. As noted by Schulz (1996), individuals are unfortunately doing what government regulations prevent many institutional investors from doing. In addition, some studies point out that the average stock allocation in many retirement plans is lower than it should be if the investor wants growth of principal over time—that is, investors tend to be too conservative. Another consideration is the issue of stock trading. A number of studies by Barber and Odean (1999, 2000, 2001) and Odean (1998, 1999) have shown that individual investors typically trade stocks too often (driving up commissions), sell stocks with gains too early (prior to further price increases), and hold on to losers too long (as the price continues to fall). These costly mistakes are especially true for men and online traders. Investors, in general, seem to neglect that important first step to achieve financial success: They do not plan for the future. Studies of retirement plans discussed by Ruffenach (2001) and Clements (1997a, b, c) show that Americans are not saving enough to finance their retirement years and they are not planning sufficiently for what will happen to their savings after they retire. Around 25 percent of workers have saved less than $50,000 for their retirement. Finally, about 60 percent of workers surveyed confessed they were "behind schedule" in planning and saving for retirement. 2.6 THE IMPORTANCE OF ASSET ALLOCATION A major reason why investors develop policy statements is to provide guidance for an overall investment strategy. Though a policy statement does not indicate which specific securities to purchase and when they should be sold, it should provide guidelines as to the asset classes to include and a range of percents of the investor's funds to invest in each class. How the investor divides funds into different asset classes is the process of asset allocation. Rather than Chapter 2: The Asset Allocation Decision 49 WWW.YAZDANPRESS.COM provide strict percentages, asset allocation is usually expressed in ranges. This allows the investment manager some freedom, based on his or her reading of capital market trends, to invest toward the upper or lower end of the ranges. For example, suppose a policy statement requires that common stocks be 60 percent to 80 percent of the value of the portfolio and that bonds should be 20 percent to 40 percent of the portfolio's value. If a manager is particularly bullish about stocks, she will increase the allocation of stocks toward the 80 percent upper end of the equity range and decrease bonds toward the 20 percent lower end of the bond range. Should she be optimistic about bonds or bearish on stocks, that manager may shift the allocation closer to 40 percent invested in bonds with the remainder in equities. A review of historical data and empirical studies provides strong support for the contention that the asset allocation decision is a critical component of the portfolio management process. In general, there are four decisions involved in constructing an investment strategy: • What asset classes should be considered for investment? • What policy weights should be assigned to each eligible asset class? • What are the allowable allocation ranges based on policy weights? • What specific securities or funds should be purchased for the portfolio? The asset allocation decision involves the first three points. How important is the asset allocation decision to an investor? In a word, very. Several studies by Ibbotson and Kaplan (2000); Brinson, Hood, and Beebower (1986); and Brinson, Singer, and Beebower (1991) have examined the effect of the normal policy weights on investment performance, using data from both pension funds and mutual funds, during time periods extending from the early 1970s to the late 1990s. The studies all found similar results: About 90 percent of a fund's returns over time can be explained by its target asset allocation policy. Exhibit 2.7 shows the relationship between returns on the target or policy portfolio allocation and actual returns on a sample mutual fund. Rather than looking at just one fund and how the target asset allocation determines its returns, some studies have looked at how much the asset allocation policy affects returns on a variety of funds with different target weights. For example, Ibbotson and Kaplan (2000) found that, across a sample of funds, about 40 percent of the difference in fund returns is explained by differences in asset allocation policy. And what does asset allocation tell us about the level of a particular fund's returns? The studies by Brinson and colleagues (1986, 1991) and Ibbotson and Kaplan (2000) answered that question as well. They divided the policy return (what the fund return would have been had it been invested in indexes at the policy weights) by the actual fund return (which includes the effects of varying from the policy weights and security selection). Thus, a fund that was passively invested at the target weights would have a ratio value of 1.0, or 100 percent. A fund managed by someone with skill in market timing (for moving in and out of asset classes) and security selection would have a ratio less than 1.0 (or less than 100 percent); the manager's skill would result in a policy return less than the actual fund return. The studies showed the opposite: The policy-return/actual-return ratio averaged over 1.0, showing that asset allocation explains slightly more than 100 percent of the level of a fund's returns. Because of market efficiency, fund managers practicing market timing and security selection, on average, have difficulty surpassing passively invested index returns, after taking into account the expenses and fees of investing. Thus, asset allocation is a very important decision. Across all funds, the asset allocation decision explains an average of 40 percent of the variation in fund returns. For a single fund, asset allocation explains 90 percent of the fund's variation in returns over time and slightly more than 100 percent of the average fund's level of return. Good investment managers may add some value to portfolio performance, but the major source of investment return—and risk—over time is the asset allocation decision (Brown, 2000). 50 Part 1: The Investment Background 2.6.1 Investment Returns after Taxes and Inflation Exhibit 2.8 provides additional historical perspectives on returns. It indicates how an investment of $1 would have grown over the

1986–2010 period and, using fairly conservative assumptions, examines how investment returns are affected by taxes and inflation. Focusing first on stocks, funds invested in 1986 in the Standard & Poor's 500 stocks would have averaged an 11.57 percent annual return through 2010. Unfortunately, this return is unrealistic because if the funds were invested over time, taxes would have to be paid and inflation would erode the real purchasing power of the invested funds. Except for tax-exempt investors and tax-deferred accounts, annual tax payments reduce investment returns. Incorporating taxes into the analysis lowers the after-tax average annual return of a stock investment to 8.33 percent. But the major reduction in the value of our investment is caused by inflation. The real after-tax average annual return on a stock over this time frame was only 5.50 percent, which is less than half our initial unadjusted 11.57 percent return!

2.6.2 Returns and Risks of Different Asset Classes By focusing on returns, we have ignored its partner—risk. Assets with higher long-term returns have these returns to compensate for their risk. Exhibit 2.9 illustrates returns (unadjusted forinflation, transaction costs and taxes) for several asset classes over time. As expected, the higher returns available from equities (both large cap and small cap) also include higher risk. This is precisely why investors need a policy statement and why the investor and manager must understand the capital markets and have a disciplined approach to investing. Safe Treasury bills will sometimes outperform equities, and, because of their higher risk, common stocks will sometimes lose significant value. These are times when undisciplined and uneducated investors become frustrated, sell their stocks at a loss, and vow never to invest in equities again. In contrast, these are just the times when disciplined investors stick to their investment plan and position their portfolios for the next bull market.5 By holding on to their stocks and continuing to purchasing more at depressed prices, the equity portion of the portfolio will experience a substantial increase in the future. The asset allocation decision determines to a great extent both the returns and the volatility of the portfolio. As noted, Exhibit 2.9 indicates that stocks are riskier than bonds or T-bills. Exhibit 2.10 shows that stocks have sometimes experienced returns lower than those of T-bills for extended periods of time. Still, the long-term results in Exhibit 2.9 show that sticking with an investment policy through difficult times provides attractive rates of return over long holding periods.6 One popular way to measure risk is to examine the variability of returns over time by computing a standard deviation or variance of annual rates of return for an asset class. This measure, which is used in Exhibit 2.9, indicates that stocks are relatively risky and T-bills are relatively safe. Another intriguing measure of risk is the probability of not meeting your investment return objective. From this perspective, the results in Exhibit 2.10 show that if the investor has a long time horizon (i.e., approaching 20 years), the risk of equities is small and that of T-bills is large because of their differences in long-term expected returns. 2.6.3 Asset Allocation Summary A carefully constructed policy statement determines the types of assets that should be included in a portfolio. The asset allocation decision, not the selection of specific stocks and bonds, determines most of the portfolio's returns over time. Although seemingly risky, investors seeking capital appreciation, income, or even capital preservation over long time periods should stipulate a sizable allocation to the equity portion in their portfolio. As noted in this section, a strategy's risk depends on the investor's goals and time horizon. As demonstrated, investing in T-bills may actually be a riskier strategy than investing in common stocks due to the risk of not meeting long-term investment return goals especially after considering the impact of inflation and taxes. Asset Allocation and Cultural Differences Thus far, our analysis has focused on U.S. investors. Non-U.S. investors make their asset allocation decisions in much the same manner; but because they face different social, economic, political, and tax environments, their allocation decisions differ from those of U.S. investors. Exhibit 2.11 shows the equity allocations of pension funds in several countries. As shown, the equity allocations vary dramatically from 79 percent in Hong Kong to 37 percent in Japan and only 8 percent in Germany. National demographic and economic differences can explain much of the divergent portfolio allocations. Of these six nations, the average age of the population is highest in Germany and Japan and lowest in the United States and the United Kingdom, which helps explain the greater use of equities in the United States and United Kingdom. Further, government privatization programs during the 1980s in the United Kingdom encouraged equity ownership among individual and institutional investors. In Germany, regulations prevent insurance firms from having more than 20 percent of their assets in equities. Both Germany and Japan have banking sectors that invest privately in firms and whose officers sit on corporate boards. Since 1980, the cost of living in the United Kingdom has increased at a rate about two times that of Germany and this inflationary bias in the U.K. economy again favors higher equity allocations. Exhibit 2.12

shows the positive relationship between the level of inflation in a country and its pension fund allocation to equity. These results and many others that could be mentioned indicate that some legislation, the general economic environment, and the demographics of a country have an effect on the asset allocation by the investors in the country.

Objectives and Constraints of Institutional Investors Institutional investors manage large amounts of funds in the course of their business. They include mutual funds, pension funds, insurance firms, endowments, and banks. In this appendix, we review the characteristics of various institutional investors and discuss their typical investment objectives and constraints. Mutual Funds A mutual fund pools sums of money from investors, which are then invested in financial assets. Each mutual fund has its own investment objective, such as capital appreciation, high current income, or money market income. A mutual fund will state its investment objective, and investors choose the funds in which to invest. Two basic constraints face mutual funds: those created by law to protect mutual fund investors and those that represent choices made by the mutual fund's managers. Some of these constraints will be discussed in the mutual fund's prospectus, which must be given to all prospective investors before they purchase shares in a mutual fund. Mutual funds are discussed in more detail in Chapter 24. Pension Funds Pension funds are a major component of retirement planning for individuals. As of 2011, U.S. pension assets were nearly $21 trillion. Basically, a firm's pension fund receives contributions from the firm, its employees, or both. The funds are invested with the purpose of giving workers either a lump-sum payment or the promise of an income stream after their retirement. Defined benefit pension plans promise to pay retirees a specific income stream after retirement. The size of the benefit is usually based on factors that include the worker's salary, or time of service, or both. The company contributes a certain amount each year to the pension plan; the size of the contribution depends on assumptions concerning future salary increases and the rate of return to be earned on the plan's assets. Under a defined benefit plan, the company carries the risk of paying the future pension benefit to retirees; should investment performance be poor, or should the company be unable to make adequate contributions to the plan, the shortfall must be made up in future years. "Poor" investment performance means the actual return on the plan's assets fell below the assumed actuarial rate of return. The actuarial rate is the discount rate used to find the present value of the plan's future obligations and thus this rate determines the size of the firm's annual contribution to the pension plan. Defined contribution pension plans do not promise set benefits but only specified contributions to the plan. As a result, employees' benefits depend on the size of the contributions made to the pension fund and the returns earned on the fund's investments. Thus, the plan's risk related to the rates of return on investments is borne by the employee. Unlike a defined benefit plan, employees' retirement income is not an obligation of the firm. A pension plan's objectives and constraints depend on whether the plan is a defined benefit plan or a defined contribution plan. We review each separately below. Defined Benefit The plan's risk tolerance depends on the plan's funding status and its actuarial rate. For underfunded plans (where the present value of the fund's liabilities to employees exceeds the value of the fund's assets), a more conservative approach toward risk is taken to ensure that the funding gap is closed over time. This may entail a strategy whereby the firm makes larger plan contributions and assumes a lower actuarial rate. Overfunded plans (where the present value of the pension liabilities is less than the plan's assets) allow a more aggressive investment strategy, which implies a higher actuarial rate. This allows the firm to reduce its contributions and increases the risk exposure of the plan. The return objective is to meet the 5 8 WWW.YAZDANPRESS.COM plan's actuarial rate of return, which is set by actuaries who estimate future pension obligations based on assumptions about future salary increases, current salaries, retirement patterns, worker life expectancies, and the firm's benefit formula. Obviously, the actuarial rate helps determine the size of the firm's plan contributions over time. The liquidity constraint on defined benefit funds is mainly a function of the average age of employees. A younger employee base means less liquidity is needed; an older employee base generally means more liquidity is needed to pay current pension obligations to retirees. The time horizon constraint is also affected by the average age of employees, although some experts recommend using a 5- to 10-year horizon for planning purposes. Taxes are not a major concern to the plan, because pension plans are exempt from paying tax on investment returns. The major legal constraint is that the plan must be run in accordance with the Employee Retirement and Income Security Act (ERISA), and investments must satisfy the "prudent-expert" standard when evaluated in the context of the overall pension plan's portfolio. Defined Contribution Notably, the individual employee decides how his or her contributions to the plan are to be invested. As a result, the objectives and constraints for defined contribution plans depend on the individual. Because the employee carries the risk of inadequate retirement funding rather than the firm, defined contribution plans are generally more conservatively invested (the majority of research indicates that employees tend to be too conservative). If, however, the plan is considered part of an estate planning tool for a wealthy founder or officer of the firm, a higher risk tolerance and return objective are appropriate because most of the plan's assets will ultimately be owned by the individual's heirs. The liquidity and time horizon needs for the plan differ depending on the average age of the individual employees and the degree of employee turnover within the firm. Similar to defined benefit plans, defined contribution plans are tax-exempt and are governed by the provisions of ERISA. Endowment Funds Endowment funds arise from contributions made to charitable or educational institutions. Rather than immediately spending the funds, the organization invests the money for the purpose of providing a future stream of income to the organization. The investment policy of an endowment fund is the result of a "tension" between the organization's need for current income and the desire for a growing future stream of income to protect against inflation. To meet the institution's operating budget needs, the fund's return objective is often set by adding the spending rate (the amount taken out of the funds each year) and the expected inflation rate. Funds that have more risk-tolerant trustees may have a higher spending rate than those overseen by more risk-averse trustees. Because a total return approach usually serves to meet the return objective over time, the organization is generally withdrawing both income and capital gain returns to meet budgeted needs. The risk tolerance of an endowment fund is largely affected by the collective risk tolerance of the organization's trustees. Due to the fund's long-term time horizon, liquidity requirements are minor except for the need to spend part of the endowment each year and maintain a cash reserve for emergencies. Many endowments are tax-exempt, although income from some private foundations can be taxed at either a 1 percent or 2 percent rate. Short-term capital gains are taxable, but long-term capital gains are not. Regulatory and legal constraints arise on the state level, where most endowments are regulated. Unique needs and preferences may affect investment strategies, especially among college or religious endowments, which may have strong preferences about social investing issues. Insurance Companies The investment objectives and constraints for an insurance company depend on whether it is a life insurance company or a nonlife (such as a property and casualty) insurance firm. Chapter 2: The Asset Allocation Decision 59 WWW.YAZDANPRESS.COM Life Insurance Companies Except for firms dealing only in term life insurance, life insurance firms collect premiums during a person's lifetime that must be invested until a death benefit is paid to the insurance contract's beneficiaries. At any time, the insured can turn in her policy and receive its cash surrender value. Discussing investment policy for an insurance firm is also complicated by the insurance industry's proliferation of insurance and quasi-investment products. Basically, an insurance company wants to earn a positive "spread," which is the difference between the rate of return on investment minus the rate of return it credits its various policyholders. This concept is similar to a defined benefit pension fund that tries to earn a rate of return in excess of its actuarial rate. If the spread is positive, the insurance firm's surplus reserve account rises; if not, the surplus account declines by an amount reflecting the negative spread. A growing surplus is an important competitive tool for life insurance companies. Attractive investment returns allow the company to advertise better policy returns than those of its competitors. A growing surplus also allows the firm to offer new products and expand insurance volume. Because life insurance companies are quasi-trust funds for savings, fiduciary principles limit the risk tolerance of the invested funds. The National Association of Insurance Commissioners (NAIC) establishes risk categories for bonds and stocks; companies with excessive investments in higher-risk categories must set aside extra funds in a mandatory securities valuation reserve (MSVR) to protect policyholders against losses. Insurance companies' liquidity needs have increased over the years due to increases in policy surrenders and product-mix changes. A company's time horizon depends upon its specific product mix. Life insurance policies require longer-term investments, whereas guaranteed insurance contracts (GICs) and shorter-term annuities require shorter investment time horizons. Tax rules changed considerably for insurance firms in the 1980s. For tax purposes, investment returns are divided into two components: first, the policyholder's share, which is the return portion covering the actuarially assumed rate of return needed to fund reserves; and second, the balance that is transferred to reserves. Unlike pensions and endowments, life insurance firms pay income and capital gains taxes at the corporate tax rates on the returns transferred to reserves. Except for the NAIC, most insurance regulation is on the state level. Regulators oversee the eligible asset classes and the reserves (MSVR) necessary for each asset class and enforce the "prudent-expert" investment standard. Audits ensure that various accounting rules and investment regulations are followed. Nonlife Insurance Companies Cash outflows are somewhat predictable for life insurance firms, based on their mortality tables. In contrast, the cash flows required by major accidents, disasters, and lawsuit settlements are not as predictable for nonlife insurance firms. Due to their fiduciary responsibility to claimants, risk exposures are low to moderate. Depending on the specific company and competitive pressures, premiums may be affected by both the probability of a claim and the investment returns earned by the firm. Typically, casualty insurance firms invest their insurance reserves in relatively safe bonds to provide needed income to pay claims; capital and surplus funds are invested in equities for their growth potential. As with life insurers, property and casualty firms have a stronger competitive position when their surplus accounts are larger than those of their competitors. Many insurers now focus on a total return objective as a means to increase their surplus accounts over time. Because of uncertain claim patterns, liquidity is a concern for property and casualty insurers who also want liquidity so they can switch between taxable and tax-exempt investments as their underwriting activities generate losses and profits. The time horizon for investments is typically shorter than that of life insurers, although many invest in long-term bonds to earn the higher yields available on these instruments. Investing strategy for the firm's surplus account focuses on long-term growth. 60 Part 1: The Investment Background WWW.YAZDANPRESS.COM Regulation of property and casualty firms is more permissive than for life insurers. Similar to life companies, states regulate classes and quality of investments for a certain percentage of the firm's assets. Beyond this restriction, insurers can invest in many different types and qualities of instruments, although some states limit the proportion that can be invested in real estate assets. Banks Pension funds, endowments, and insurance firms obtain virtually free funds for investment purposes. Not so with banks. To have funds to lend, they must attract investors in a competitive interest rate environment. They compete against other banks and also against companies that offer other investment vehicles, from bonds to common stocks. A bank's success relies primarily on its ability to generate returns in excess of its funding costs. A bank tries to maintain a positive difference between its cost of funds and its returns on assets. If banks anticipate falling interest rates, they will try to invest in longer-term assets to lock in the returns while seeking short-term deposits, whose interest cost is expected to fall over time. When banks expect rising rates, they will try to lock in longer-term deposits with fixed-interest costs, while investing funds short term to capture rising interest rates. The risk of such strategies is that losses may occur should a bank incorrectly forecast the direction of interest rates. The aggressiveness of a bank's strategy will be related to the size of its capital ratio and the oversight of regulators. Banks need substantial liquidity to meet withdrawals and loan demand. A bank has two forms of liquidity. Internal liquidity is provided by a bank's investment portfolio that includes highly liquid assets. A bank hasexternal liquidity if it can borrow funds in the federal funds markets (where banks lend reserves to other banks), from the Federal Reserve Bank's discount window, or if it can sell certificates of deposit at attractive rates. Banks have a short time horizon for several reasons. First, they have a strong need for liquidity. Second, because they want to maintain an adequate interest revenue–interest expense spread, they generally focus on shorter-term investments to avoid interest rate risk and to avoid getting "locked in" to a long-term revenue source. Third, because banks typically offer short-term deposit accounts (demand deposits, NOW accounts, and such) they need to match the maturity of their assets and liabilities to avoid taking undue risks. This desire to match the maturity of assets and liabilities is shared by virtually all financial institutions. Banks are heavily regulated by numerous state and federal agencies. The Federal Reserve Board, the Comptroller of the Currency, and the Federal Deposit Insurance Corporation all oversee various components of bank operations. The Glass-Steagall Act restricts the equity investments that banks can make. Unique situations that affect each bank's investment policy depend on their size, market, and management skills in matching asset and liability sensitivity to interest rates. For example, a bank in a small community may have many customers who deposit their money with it for the sake of convenience. A bank in a more populated area will find its deposit flows are more sensitive to interest rates and competition from nearby banks. Institutional Investment Summary Among the great variety of institutions, each institution has its "typical" investment objectives and constraints. This discussion has indicated the differences that exist among types of institutions and some of the major issues confronting them. Notably, just as with individual investors, "cookie-cutter" policy statements are inappropriate for institutional investors. The specific objectives, constraints, and investment strategies must be determined on a case-bycase basis.

CHAPTER FOUR

Selecting Investments in a Global Market

Individuals are willing to defer current consumption for many reasons. Some save for their children's college tuition or their own; others wish to accumulate down payments for a home, car, or boat; others want to amass adequate retirement funds for the future. Whatever the reasons for an investment program, the techniques we used in Chapter 1 to measure risk and return will help you evaluate alternative investments. But what are those alternative investments? Thus far, we have said little about the investment opportunities available in financial markets. In this chapter, we address this issue by surveying investment alternatives. This is essential background for making the asset allocation decision discussed in Chapter 2 and for later chapters where we analyze several individual investments, such as bonds, common stock, and other securities. It is also important when we consider how to construct and evaluate portfolios of investments. As an investor in the 21st century, you have an array of investment choices unavailable a few decades ago. As discussed by Miller (1991), a combination of dynamic financial markets, technological advances, and new regulations have resulted in numerous new investment instruments and expanded trading opportunities. Improvements in communications and relaxation of international regulations have made it easier for investors to trade in both domestic and global markets. Telecommunications networks enable U.S. brokers to reach security exchanges in London, Tokyo, and other European and Asian cities as easily as those in New York, Chicago, and other U.S. cities. The competitive environment in the brokerage industry and the deregulation of the banking sector have made it possible for more financial institutions to compete for investor dollars.

All of his has spawned investment vehicles with a variety of maturities, risk-return characteristics, and cash flow patterns. In this chapter, we examine some of these choices. As an investor, you need to understand the differences among investments so you can build a properly diversified portfolio that conforms to your objectives. That is, you should seek to acquire a group of investments with different patterns of returns over time. If chosen carefully, such portfolios minimize risk for a given level of return because low or negative rates of return on some investments during a period of time are offset by above-average returns on others. Your goal should be to build a balanced portfolio of investments with relatively stable overall rates of return. A major goal of this text is to help you understand and evaluate the risk-return characteristics of investment portfolios. An appreciation of alternative security types is the starting point for this analysis. This chapter is divided into three main sections. Because investors can choose securities from around the world, we initially look at a combination of reasons why investors should include foreign as well as domestic securities in their portfolios. Taken together, these reasons provide a compelling case for global investing. In the second section of this chapter, we discuss securities in domestic and global markets, describing their main features and cash flow patterns. You will see that the varying risk-return characteristics of alternative investments suit the preferences of different investors. The third and final section contains the historical risk and return performance of several investment instruments from around the world and examines the relationship among the returns for many of these securities. These results provide strong empirical support for global investing

3.1 THE CASE FOR GLOBAL INVESTMENTS Twenty years ago, the bulk of investments available to individual investors consisted of U.S. stocks and bonds. Now, however, a call to your broker gives you access to a wide range of securities sold throughout the world. Currently, you can purchase stock in General Motors or Toyota, U.S. Treasury bonds or Japanese government bonds, a mutual fund that invests in U.S. biotechnology companies, a global growth stock fund, a German or Chinese stock fund, or options on a U.S. stock index. Several changes have caused this explosion of investment opportunities. For one, the growth and development of numerous foreign financial markets, such as those in Japan, the United Kingdom, and Germany, as well as emerging markets, such as China and India, have made these markets accessible and viable for investors around the world. U.S. investment firms have recognized this opportunity and established facilities in these countries aided by advances in telecommunications technology that allow constant contact with offices and financial markets around the world. In addition to the efforts by U.S. firms, foreign firms and investors undertook counterbalancing initiatives, including significant mergers of firms and security exchanges. As a result, as described by Pardee (1987), investors and investment firms can easily trade securities in markets around the world. There are three interrelated reasons U.S. investors should think of constructing global investment portfolios: 1. When investors compare the absolute and relative sizes of U.S. and foreign markets for stocks and bonds, they see that ignoring foreign markets reduces their choices to less than 50 percent of available investment opportunities. Because more opportunities broaden your range of risk-return choices, it makes sense to evaluate foreign securities when selecting investments and building a portfolio. 2. The rates of return available on non-U.S. securities often have substantially exceeded those for U.S.-only securities. The higher returns on non-U.S. equities can be justified by the higher growth rates for the countries where they are issued. 3. A major tenet of investment theory is that investors should diversify their portfolios. Because the relevant factor when diversifying a portfolio is low correlation between asset returns over time, diversification with foreign securities that have very low correlation with U.S. securities can substantially reduce portfolio risk. In this section, we analyze these reasons to demonstrate the advantages to a growing role of foreign financial markets for U.S. investors and to assess the benefits and risks of trading in these markets. Notably, the reasons that global investing is appropriate for U.S. investors are generally even more compelling for non-U.S. investors. 3.1.1 Relative Size of U.S. Financial Markets Prior to 1970, the securities traded in the U.S. stock and bond markets comprised about 65 percent of all the securities available in world capital markets. Therefore, a U.S. investor selecting securities strictly from U.S. markets had a fairly complete set of investments available. Under these conditions, most U.S. investors probably believed that it was not worth the time and effort to expand their investment universe to include the limited investments available in foreign markets. That situation has changed dramatically over the past 40 plus years. Currently, investors who ignore foreign stock and bond markets limit their investment choices substantially. Exhibit 3.1 shows the breakdown of securities available in world capital markets in 1969 and 2010. Not only has the overall value of all securities increased dramatically (from $2.3 trillion to $113.6 trillion), but the composition has also changed. Concentrating on proportions of bond and equity investments, the exhibit shows that in 1969 U.S. dollar bonds and U.S. equity securities made up 53 percent of the total value of all securities versus 28.4 percent for the total of nondollar bonds and equity. By 2010, U.S. bonds and equities accounted for 42.6 percent of the total securities market versus 47.2 percent for nondollar bonds and stocks. These data indicate that if you consider only the U.S. proportion of this combined stock and bond market, it has declined from 65 percent of the total in 1969 to about 47 percent in 2010. The point is, the U.S. security markets now include a substantially smaller proportion of the total world capital market, and this trend will almost certainly continue. The faster economic growth of many other countries compared to the United States will require foreign governments and individual companies to issue debt and equity securities to finance this growth. Therefore, U.S. investors should consider investing in foreign securities because of the growing importance of these foreign securities in world capital markets. Put another way, not investing in foreign stocks and bonds means you are ignoring over 50 percent of the securities that are available to you. This approximate 50–50 breakdown is about the same for bonds alone, while U.S. stocks are only about 42 percent of global stocks. 3.1.2 Rates of Return on U.S. and Foreign Securities An examination of the rates of return on U.S. and foreign securities not only demonstrates that many non-U.S. securities provide superior rates of return but also shows the impact of the exchange rate risk discussed in Chapter 1. Global Bond-Market Returns Exhibit 3.2 reports annual rates of return for several major international bond markets for 1986–2010. The returns have been converted to U.S. dollar returns, so the exhibit shows mean annual returns and standard deviations that a U.S.-based investor would receive. An analysis of the returns in Exhibit 3.2 indicates that the return performance of the U.S. bond market ranked fifth out of the six countries. Part of the reason for the better performance in dollar terms of the non-U.S. markets is that the dollar generally weakened during this time frame, giving U.S. investors a boost to their foreign returns. Put another way, U.S. investors who invested in these foreign bonds received the return on the bonds equal to that of local investors, but also received a return for holding the foreign currency that appreciated relative to the U.S. dollar. Global Equity-Market Returns Exhibit 3.3 shows the annual returns in U.S. dollars for 34 major equity markets yearly from 2007 through 2010. The United States' average rank in U.S. dollar returns in 2007–2010 was 17.5

out of 34 countries (and it was only in the top 10 once). Its performance was typically behind the returns of numerous stock markets in these years. These results for equity and bond markets around the world indicate that investors who limit themselves to the U.S. market may well experience rates of return below those in many other countries. 3.1.3 Risk of Combined Country Investments Thus far, we have discussed the risk and return results for individual countries. In Chapter 1, we considered the idea of combining a number of assets into a portfolio and noted that investors should create diversified portfolios to reduce the variability of the returns over time. We discussed how proper diversification reduces the variability (our measure of risk) of the portfolio because alternative investments have different patterns of returns over time. Specifically, when the rates of return on some investments are negative or below average, potentially other investments in the portfolio will be experiencing above-average rates of return. Therefore, if a portfolio is properly diversified, it should provide a more stable rate of return for the total portfolio (that is, it will have a lower standard deviation and therefore less risk). Although we will discuss and demonstrate portfolio theory .

The way to measure whether two investments will contribute to diversifying a portfolio is to compute the correlation coefficient between their rates of return over time. Correlation coefficients can range from +1.00 to −1.00. A correlation of +1.00 means that the rates of return for these two investments move exactly together. Combining investments that move exactly together in a portfolio would not help diversify the portfolio because they have identical rate-of-return patterns over time. In contrast, a correlation coefficient of −1.00 means that the rates of return for two investments move exactly opposite to each other. When one investment is experiencing above-average rates of return, the other is suffering through similar below-average rates of return. Combining two investments with large negative correlation in a portfolio would be ideal for diversification because it would stabilize the rates of return over time, reducing the standard deviation of the portfolio rates of return and hence the risk of the portfolio. Therefore, if you want to diversify your portfolio and reduce your risk, you want an investment that has either low positive correlation, zero correlation, or, ideally, negative correlation with the other investments in your portfolio. With this in mind, the following discussion considers the correlations of returns among U.S. bonds and stocks with the returns on foreign bonds and stocks. Global Bond Portfolio Risk Exhibit 3.4 lists the correlation coefficients between rates of return for bonds in the United States and bonds in major foreign markets in U.S. dollar terms from 1986–2010. For a U.S. investor, these important correlations averaged only 0.58. These relatively low positive correlations among returns in U.S. dollars mean that U.S. investors have substantial opportunities for risk reduction through global diversification of bond portfolios. A U.S. investor who bought bonds in these non-U.S. markets especially Japan would reduce the standard deviation of a well-diversified U.S. bond portfolio. Why do these correlation coefficients for returns between U.S. bonds and those of various foreign countries differ? That is, why is the U.S.-Canada correlation 0.75, whereas the U.S.- Japan correlation is only 0.34? The answer is because the international trade patterns, economic growth, fiscal policies, and monetary policies of the countries differ. We do not have an integrated world economy but, rather, a collection of economies that are related to one another in different ways. As an example, the U.S. and Canadian economies are closely related because of their geographic proximity, similar domestic economic policies, and the extensive trade between them. Each is the other's largest trading partner. In contrast, the United States has less trade with Japan and the fiscal and monetary policies of the two countries differ dramatically. For example, the U.S. economy was growing during much of the 1990s while the Japanese economy experienced a prolonged recession. The point is, macroeconomic differences cause the correlation of bond returns between the United States and each country to likewise differ. These differing correlations make it worth-while to diversify with foreign bonds, and the different correlations indicate which countries will provide the greatest reduction in the standard deviation (risk) of bond portfolio returns for a U.S. investor. Also, the correlation of returns between a single pair of countries changes over time because the factors influencing the correlations, such as international trade, economic growth, fiscal policy, and monetary policy, change over time. A change in any of these variables will produce a change in how the economies are related and a change in the relationship between returns on bonds. For example, the correlation in U.S. dollar returns between U.S. and Japanese bonds was 0.07 in the late 1960s and 1970s; it was 0.35 in the 1980s and 0.25 in the 1990s but only about 0.30 in the 2000–2010 time frame. Exhibit 3.5 shows what happens to the risk-return trade-off when we combine U.S. and foreign bonds. A comparison of a completely non-U.S. portfolio (100 percent foreign) and a 100 percent U.S. portfolio indicates that the non-U.S. portfolio has both a higher rate of return and a higher standard deviation of returns than the U.S. portfolio. Combining the two portfolios in different proportions provides an interesting set of points. As we will discuss in Chapter 7, the expected rate of return is a weighted average of the two portfolios. In contrast, the risk (standard deviation) of the combination is not a weighted average but also depends on the correlation between the two portfolios. In this example, the risk levels of the combined portfolios decline below those of the individual portfolios. Therefore, by adding foreign bonds that have low correlation with a portfolio of U.S. bonds, a U.S. investor is able to not only increase the expected rate of return but also reduce the risk compared to a total U.S. bond portfolio.

of each country and the U.S. market for the period from 1988 to 2010. Only 4 of the 11 correlations between U.S. dollar returns were over 0.70, and the average correlation was only 0.65. These relatively small positive correlations between U.S. stocks and foreign stocks have similar implications to those derived for bonds. Investors can reduce the overall risk of their stock portfolios by including foreign stocks. Exhibit 3.7 demonstrates the impact of international equity diversification. These curves demonstrate that, as you increase the number of randomly selected securities in a portfolio, the standard deviation will decline due to the benefits of diversification within your own country. This is referred to as domestic diversification. After a certain number of securities (40 to 50), the curve will flatten out at a risk level that reflects the basic market risk for the domestic economy (see Campbell, Lettau, Malkiel, and Xu [2001]). The lower curve illustrates the benefits of international diversification. This curve demonstrates that adding foreign securities to a U.S. portfolio to create a global portfolio enables an investor to experience lower overall risk because the non-U.S. securities are not correlated with our economy or our stock market, allowing the investor to eliminate some of the basic market risks of the U.S. economy. To see how this works, consider, for example, the effect of inflation and interest rates on all U.S. securities. As discussed in Chapter 1, all U.S. securities will be affected by these variables. In contrast, a Japanese stock is mainly affected by what happens in the Japanese economy and will typically not be affected by changes in U.S. variables. Thus, adding Japanese, Australian, and Italian stocks to a U.S. stock portfolio reduces the portfolio risk of the global portfolio to a level that reflects only worldwide systematic factors. Summary on Global Investing At this point, we have considered the relative size of the market for non-U.S. bonds and stocks and found that it has grown in size and importance, becoming too big to ignore. We have also examined the rates of return for foreign bond and stock investments and determined that, when considering results, their rates of return were often superior to those in the U.S. market. Finally, we discussed constructing a portfolio of investments and the importance of diversification in reducing the variability of returns over time, which reduces the risk of the portfolio. As noted, to have successful diversification, an investor should combine investments with low positive or negative correlations between rates of return. An analysis of the correlation between rates of return on U.S. and foreign bonds and stocks indicated a consistent pattern of relatively low positive correlations. Therefore, the existence of similar rates of return on foreign securities combined with low correlation coefficients indicates that adding foreign stocks and bonds to a U.S. portfolio will almost certainly reduce the risk of the portfolio and can possibly increase its average return. Given the several compelling reasons for adding foreign securities to a U.S. portfolio, investors should develop a global investment perspective because this approach is clearly justified, and this trend toward global investing is expected to continue. Implementing this new global investment perspective will not be easy because it requires an understanding of new terms, instruments (such as Eurobonds), and institutions (such as non-U.S. stock and bond markets). Still, the effort is justified because you are developing a set of skills and a way of thinking that will enhance your long-term investing results. The next section presents an overview of investment alternatives from around the world, beginning with fixed-income investments and progressing through numerous alternatives. 3.2 GLOBAL INVESTMENT CHOICES This section provides an important foundation for subsequent chapters in which we describe techniques to value individual investments and combine alternative investments into properly diversified portfolios that conform to your risk-return objectives. In this section, we briefly describe the numerous investment alternatives available. This survey introduces each of these investment alternatives so you can appreciate the full spectrum of opportunities. Most of these assets will be described in greater detail in subsequent chapters. The investments are divided by asset classes. First, we describe fixed-income investments, including bonds and preferred stocks. In the second subsection, we discuss equity investments, and the third subsection contains a discussion of special equity instruments, such as warrants and options, which have characteristics of both fixed-income and equity instruments. In subsection four, we consider futures contracts that allow for a wide range of return-risk profiles. The fifth subsection considers investment companies. All these investments are called financial assets because their payoffs are in money. In contrast, real assets, such as real estate, are discussed in the sixth subsection. We conclude with assets that are considered low liquidity investments because of the relative difficulty in buying and selling them. This includes art, antiques, coins, stamps, and precious gems. The final section of the chapter presents the historical return and risk patterns for many individual investment alternatives and the correlations among the returns for these investments. This additional background and perspective will help you evaluate individual investments in order to build a properly diversified portfolio of global investments. 3.2.1 Fixed-Income Investments Fixed-income investments have a contractually mandated payment schedule. Their investment contracts promise specific payments at predetermined times, although the legal force behind the promise varies and this affects their risks and required returns. At one extreme, if the issuing firm does not make its payment at the appointed time, creditors can declare the issuing firm in default. In other cases (for example, income bonds), the issuing firm must make payments only if it earns profits. In yet other instances (for example, preferred stock), the issuing firm does not have to make dividend payments unless its board of directors votes to do so. Investors who acquire fixed-income securities (except preferred stock) are really lenders to the issuers. Specifically, you lend some amount of money, the principal, to the borrower. In return, the borrower typically promises to make periodic interest payments and to pay back the principal at the maturity of the loan. Savings Accounts You might not think of savings accounts as fixed-income investments, yet an individual who deposits funds in a savings account at a financial institution is really lending money to the institution and, as a result, earning a fixed payment. These investments are considered to be convenient, liquid, and low risk because almost all are insured. Consequently, their rates of return are generally low compared with other alternatives. Several versions of these accounts have been developed to appeal to investors with differing objectives. Passbook savings accounts have no minimum balance, and funds may be withdrawn at any time with little loss of interest. Due to their flexibility, the promised interest on passbook accounts is relatively low. For investors with larger amounts of funds who are willing to give up liquidity, financial institutions developed certificates of deposit (CDs), which require minimum deposits (typically

$500) and have fixed durations (usually three months, six months, one year, two years). The promised rates on CDs are higher than those for passbook savings accounts, and the rate increases with the size and the duration of the deposit. An investor who wants to cash in a CD prior to its stated expiration date must pay a heavy penalty in the form of a much lower interest rate. Investors with large sums of money ($10,000 or more) can invest in Treasury bills (T-bills)— short-term obligations (maturing in 3–12 months) of the U.S. government. To compete against T-bills, banks issue money market certificates, which require minimum investments of $10,000 and have minimum maturities of six months. The promised rate on these certificates fluctuates at some premium over the weekly rate on six-month T-bills. Investors can redeem these certificates only at the bank of issue, and they incur penalties if they withdraw their funds before maturity. Capital Market Instruments Capital market instruments are fixed-income obligations that trade in the secondary market, which means you can buy and sell them to other individuals or institutions. Capital market instruments fall into four categories: (1) U.S. Treasury securities, (2) U.S. government agency securities, (3) municipal bonds, and (4) corporate bonds. U.S. Treasury Securities All government securities issued by the U.S. Treasury are fixedincome instruments. They may be bills, notes, or bonds depending on their initial times to maturity. Specifically, bills mature in one year or less, notes in over one to 10 years, and bonds in more than 10 years from time of issue. U.S. government obligations are essentially free of credit risk because there is little chance of default and they are highly liquid. U.S. Government Agency Securities Agency securities are sold by various agencies of the government to support specific programs, but they are not direct obligations of the Treasury. Examples of agencies that issue these bonds include the Federal National Mortgage Association (FNMA or Fannie Mae), and the Federal Home Loan Mortgage Corporation (Freddie Mac) which sells bonds and uses the proceeds to purchase mortgages from insurance companies or savings and loans; and the Federal Home Loan Bank (FHLB), which sells bonds and loans the money to its 12 banks, which in turn provide credit to savings and loans and other mortgagegranting institutions. Other agencies are the Government National Mortgage Association (GNMA or Ginnie Mae), Banks for Cooperatives, Federal Land Banks (FLBs), and the Federal Housing Administration (FHA). Although the securities issued by federal agencies (except GNMA) are not direct obligations of the government (they are not officially guaranteed by the

Treasury), they have been considered default-free because it was believed that the government would not allow them to default.1 Municipal Bonds Municipal bonds are issued by local government entities as either general obligation or revenue bonds. General obligation bonds (GOs) are backed by the full taxing power of the municipality. In contrast, revenue bonds pay the interest from revenue generated by specific projects (e.g., the revenue to pay the interest on sewer bonds comes from water taxes). Municipal bonds differ from other fixed-income securities because they are tax-exempt. The interest earned from them is exempt from taxation by the federal government and historically by some states that issued the bond, provided the investor is a resident of that state. For this reason, municipal bonds are popular with investors in high tax brackets. For an investor having a marginal tax rate of 35 percent, a regular bond with an interest rate of 8 percent yields a net return after taxes of only 5.20 percent [0.08 × (1 – 0.35)]. Such an investor would prefer a tax-free bond of equal risk with a 6 percent yield. This allows municipal bonds to offer yields that are generally 20 to 30 percent lower than yields on comparable taxable bonds. As will be discussed in Chapter 17, this relationship changed temporarily in 2010 and 2011 for several reasons. We will also discuss taxable municipal bonds. Corporate Bonds Corporate bonds are fixed-income securities issued by industrial corporations, public utility corporations, or railroads to raise funds to invest in plant, equipment, or working capital. They can be broken down by issuer (industrial or utility), in terms of credit quality (measured by the ratings assigned by an agency on the basis of probability of default), in terms of maturity (short term, intermediate term, or long term), or based on some component of the indenture (sinking fund or call feature). Historically, corporate bonds have been substantially less liquid than Treasury or agency bonds, but the difference has declined due to real-time quotes for about 6,000 bonds on the NYSE and improved acquisition alternatives, described by Kim (2007). All bonds include an indenture, which is the legal agreement that lists the obligations of the issuer to the bondholder, including the payment schedule and features such as call provisions and sinking funds. Call provisions specify when a firm can issue a call for the bonds prior to their maturity, at which time current bondholders must submit the bonds to the issuing firm, which redeems them (that is, pays back the principal and a small premium). A sinking fund provision specifies payments the issuer must make to redeem a given percentage of the outstanding issue prior to maturity. Corporate bonds fall into various categories based on their contractual promises to investors. They will be discussed in order of their seniority. Secured bonds are the most senior bonds in a firm's capital structure and have the lowest risk of distress or default. They include various secured issues that differ based on the assets that are pledged. Mortgage bonds are backed by liens on specific assets, such as land and buildings. In the case of default, the proceeds from the sale of these assets are used to pay off the mortgage bondholders. Collateral trust bonds are a form of mortgage bond except that the assets backing the bonds are financial assets, such as stocks, notes, and other high-quality bonds. Finally, equipment trust certificates are mortgage bonds that are secured by specific pieces of transportation equipment, such as locomotives and boxcars for a railroad and airplanes for an airline. Debentures are promises to pay interest and principal, but they pledge no specific assets (referred to as collateral) in case the firm does not fulfill its promise. This means that the bondholder depends on the success of the borrower to make the promised payment. Debenture owners usually have first call on the firm's earnings and any assets that are not already pledged by the firm as backing for senior secured bonds. If the issuer does not make an interest payment, the debenture owners can declare the firm bankrupt and claim any unpledged assets to pay off the bonds. Subordinated bonds are similar to debentures, but, in the case of default, subordinated bondholders have claim to the assets of the firm only after the firm has satisfied the claims of all senior secured and debenture bondholders. That is, the claims of subordinated bondholders are secondary to those of other bondholders. Within this general category of subordinated issues, you can find senior subordinated, subordinated, and junior subordinated bonds. Junior subordinated bonds have the weakest claim of all bondholders. Income bonds stipulate interest payment schedules, but the interest is due and payable only if the issuers earn the income to make the payment by stipulated dates. If the company does not earn the required amount, it does not have to make the interest payment and it cannot be declared in default. Instead, the interest payment is considered in arrears and, if subsequently earned, it must be paid off. Because the issuing firm is not legally bound to make its interest payments except when the firm earns it, an income bond is not considered as safe as a debenture or a mortgage bond, so income bonds offer higher returns to compensate investors for the added risk. There are a limited number of corporate income bonds. In contrast, income bonds are fairly popular with municipalities because municipal revenue bonds discussed previously are basically income bonds. Convertible bonds have the interest and principal characteristics of other bonds, with the added feature that the bondholder has the option to turn them back to the firm in exchange for its common stock. For example, a firm could issue a $1,000 face-value bond and stipulate that owners of the bond could turn the bond in to the issuing corporation and convert it into 40 shares of the firm's common stock. These bonds appeal to investors because they combine the features of a fixed-income security with the option of conversion into the common stock of the firm, should the firm prosper. Because of their desirable conversion option, convertible bonds generally pay lower interest rates than nonconvertible debentures of comparable risk. The difference in the required interest rate increases with the growth potential of the company because this growth potential 74 Part 1: The Investment Background WWW.YAZDANPRESS.COM increases the value of the option to convert the bonds into common stock. These bonds are almost always subordinated to the nonconvertible debt of the firm, so they are considered to have higher credit risk and receive a lower credit rating from the bond rating firms. An alternative to convertible bonds is a debenture with warrants attached. The warrant is likewise an option that allows the bondholder to purchase the firm's common stock from the firm at a specified price for a given time period. The specified purchase price for the stock set in the warrant is typically above the price of the stock at the time the firm issues the bond but below the expected future stock price. The warrant makes the debenture more desirable, which lowers its required yield. The warrant also provides the firm with future common stock capital because when the bond holder exercises the warrant, he/she buys the stock from the firm. Unlike the typical bond that pays interest every six months and its face value at maturity, a zero coupon bond promises no interest payments during the life of the bond but only the payment of the principal at maturity. Therefore, the purchase price of the bond is the present value of the principal payment at the required rate of return. For example, the price of a zero coupon bond that promises to pay $10,000 in five years with a required rate of return of 8 percent is $6,756. To find this, assuming semiannual compounding (which is the norm), use the present value factor for 10 periods at 4 percent, which is 0.6756. Preferred Stock Preferred stock is classified as a fixed-income security because its yearly payment is stipulated as either a coupon (for example, 5 percent of the face value) or a stated dollar amount (for example, $5 preferred).

Preferred stock differs from bonds because its payment is a dividend and therefore not legally binding. For each period, the firm's board of directors must vote to pay it, similar to a common stock dividend. Even if the firm earned enough money to pay the preferred stock dividend, the board of directors could theoretically vote to withhold it. Because most preferred stock is cumulative, the unpaid dividends would accumulate to be paid in full at a later time. Although preferred dividends are not legally binding, as are the interest payments on a bond, they are considered practically binding because of the credit implications of a missed dividend. Because corporations can exclude 80 percent of intercompany dividends from taxable income, preferred stocks have become attractive investments for financial corporations. For example, a corporation that owns preferred stock of another firm and receives $100 in dividends can exclude 80 percent of this amount and pay taxes on only 20 percent of it ($20). Assuming a 40 percent tax rate, the tax would only be $8 or 8 percent versus 40 percent on other investment income. Due to this tax benefit to corporations, the yield on high-grade preferred stock is typically lower than that on high-grade bonds. 3.2.2 International Bond Investing As noted earlier, more than half of all fixed-income securities available to U.S. investors are issued by firms in countries outside the United States. Investors identify these securities in different ways: by the country or city of the issuer (for example, United States, United Kingdom, Japan); by the location of the primary trading market (for example, United States, London); by the home country of the major buyers; and by the currency in which the securities are denominated (for example, dollars, yen, euros). We identify foreign bonds by their country of origin and include these other differences in each description. A Eurobond is an international bond denominated in a currency not native to the country where it is issued. Specific kinds of Eurobonds include Eurodollar bonds, Euroyen bonds, and Eurosterling bonds. A Eurodollar bond is denominated in U.S. dollars and sold outside the United States to non-U.S. investors. A specific example would be a U.S. dollar bond issued by General Electric and sold in London. Eurobonds are typically issued in Europe, with the major concentration in London. Chapter 3: Selecting Investments in a Global Market 75 WWW.YAZDANPRESS.COM Eurobonds can also be denominated in yen. For example, Nippon Steel can issue Euroyen bonds for sale in London. Also, if it appears that investors are looking for a specific foreign currency bonds, a U.S. corporation can issue a Euroyen bond in London. Yankee bonds are sold in the United States, denominated in U.S. dollars, but issued by foreign corporations or governments. This allows a U.S. citizen to buy the bond of a foreign firm or government but receive all payments in U.S. dollars, eliminating exchange rate risk. An example would be a U.S. dollar-denominated bond issued by British Airways. Similar foreign bonds are issued in other countries, including the Bulldog Market, which involves British sterling-denominated bonds issued in the United Kingdom by non-British firms, or the Samurai Market, which involves yen-denominated bonds issued in Japan by non-Japanese firms. International domestic bonds are sold by an issuer within its own country in that country's currency. An example would be a bond sold by Nippon Steel in Japan denominated in yen. A U.S. investor acquiring such a bond would receive maximum diversification but would incur the exchange rate risk of Japanese currency. 3.2.3 Equity Instruments This section describes several equity instruments, which differ from fixed-income securities because their returns are not contractual. As a result, you can receive returns that are much better or much worse than what you would receive on a bond. We begin with common stock, the most popular equity instrument and probably the most popular investment instrument. Common stock represents ownership of a firm. Owners of the common stock of a firm share in the company's successes and problems. If—like Walmart, Microsoft, Google, or Apple—the company prospers, the investor receives high rates of return and can become wealthy. In contrast, the investor can lose money if the firm does not do well or even goes bankrupt, as the once formidable K-Mart, Enron, W. T. Grant, and several U.S. airlines all did. In these instances, the firm may be forced to liquidate its assets and pay off all its creditors. Notably, the firm's preferred stockholders and common stock owners receive what is left, which is usually little or nothing. Investing in common stock entails all the advantages and disadvantages of ownership and is a relatively risky investment compared with fixed-income securities. As shown, this is reflected in relative return volatility. Common Stock Classifications When considering an investment in common stock, people tend to divide the vast universe of stocks into categories based on general business lines and by industry within these business lines. The division includes broad classifications for industrial firms, utilities, transportation firms, and financial institutions. Within each of these broad classes are specific industries. The industrial group, which is very diverse, includes such industries as automobiles, industrial machinery, chemicals, and beverages. Utilities include electrical power companies, gas suppliers, and the water industry. Transportation includes airlines, trucking firms, and railroads. Financial institutions include commercial banks, insurance companies, and investment firms. An alternative classification scheme might separate domestic (U.S.) and foreign common stocks. We avoid this division because the business line-industry breakdown is more appropriate and useful when constructing a diversified portfolio of global common stock investments. With a global capital market, the focus of analysis should include all the companies in an industry viewed in a global setting. The point is, it is not relevant whether a major chemical firm is located in the United States or Germany, just as it is not relevant whether a computer firm is located in Michigan or California. Therefore, when considering the automobile industry, it is necessary to go beyond pure U.S. auto firms like General Motors and Ford and consider auto firms from throughout the world, such as Honda Motors, Porsche, Daimler, Nissan, Toyota, and Fiat. 76 Part 1: The Investment Background WWW.YAZDANPRESS.COM Acquiring Foreign Equities We begin our discussion on foreign equities by considering how you buy and sell these securities because this procedural information has often been a major impediment. Many investors may recognize the desirability of investing in foreign common stock because of the risk and return characteristics discussed earlier, but they may be intimidated by the logistics of the transaction. This section attempts to alleviate this concern by explaining the alternatives available. Currently, there are several ways to acquire foreign common stock: 1. Purchase or sale of American Depository Receipts (ADRs) 2. Purchase or sale of American shares 3. Direct purchase or sale of foreign shares listed on a U.S. or foreign stock exchange 4. Purchase or sale of international or global mutual funds or exchange-traded funds (ETFs) Purchase or Sale of American Depository Receipts The easiest way to acquire shares of an individual foreign company directly is through American Depository Receipts (ADRs). These are certificates of ownership issued by a U.S. bank that represent indirect ownership of a certain number of shares of a specific foreign firm on deposit in a bank in the firm's home country. ADRs are a convenient way to own foreign shares because the investor buys and sells them in U.S. dollars and receives all dividends in U.S. dollars. Therefore, the price and returns reflect both the domestic returns for the stock and the exchange rate effect. Also, the price of an ADR can reflect the fact that it represents multiple shares—for example, an ADR can be for 5 or 10 shares of the foreign stock. ADRs can be issued at the discretion of a bank based on the demand for the stock. The shareholder absorbs the additional handling costs of an ADR through higher transfer expenses, which are deducted from dividend payments. ADRs are quite popular in the United States because of their diversification benefits, as documented by Wahab and Khandwala (1993). At the end of 2010, 474 foreign companies had stocks listed on the New York Stock Exchange (NYSE) and 361 of these were available through ADRs, including all the stock listed from Japan, the United Kingdom, Australia, Mexico, and the Netherlands. Purchase or Sale of American Shares American shares are securities issued in the United States by a transfer agent acting on behalf of a foreign firm. Because of the added effort and expense incurred by the foreign firm, a limited number of American shares are available. Direct Purchase or Sale of Foreign Shares The most difficult and complicated foreign equity transaction takes place in the country where the firm is located because it must be carried out in the foreign currency and the shares must then be transferred to the United States. This routine can be cumbersome. A second alternative is a transaction on a foreign stock exchange outside the country where the securities originated. For example, if you acquired shares of a French auto company listed on the London Stock Exchange (LSE), the shares would be denominated in pounds and the transfer would be swift, assuming your broker has a membership on the LSE. Finally, you could purchase foreign stocks listed on the NYSE or NASDAQ. This is similar to buying a U.S. stock, but only a limited number of foreign firms qualify for—and are willing to accept—the cost of listing. Still, this number is growing. At the end of 2010, more than 110 foreign firms (mostly Canadian) were directly listed on the NYSE, in addition to the firms that were available through ADRs. Also, many foreign firms are traded on the NASDAQ market. Purchase or Sale of Global Mutual Funds or ETFs Numerous mutual funds or exchangetraded funds (ETFs) make it possible for investors to indirectly acquire the stocks of firms from outside the United States. The alternatives range from global funds, which invest in both U.S. stocks and foreign stocks, to international funds, which invest almost wholly outside the United States. In turn, international funds can (1) diversify across many countries, Chapter 3: Selecting Investments in a Global Market 77 WWW.YAZDANPRESS.COM (2) concentrate in a segment of the world (for example, Europe, South America, the Pacific basin), (3) concentrate in a specific country (for example, the Japan Fund, the Germany Fund, the Italy Fund, or the Korea Fund), or (4) concentrate in types of markets (for example, emerging markets, which would include stocks from countries such as Thailand, Indonesia, India, and China). A mutual fund is a convenient path to global investing, particularly for a small investor, because the purchase or sale of one of these funds is similar to a transaction for a comparable U.S. stock. A recent innovation in the world of index products are exchange-traded funds (ETFs) that are depository receipts for a portfolio of securities deposited at a financial institution in a unit trust that issues a certificate of ownership for the portfolio of stocks (similar to ADRs discussed earlier). The stocks in a portfolio are those in an index like the S&P 500 or the Russell 3000 and dozens of country or specific industry indexes. As of early 2011, Barron's had a separate listing of "Exchange Traded Portfolios" that contained almost 900 different portfolios to consider (about 70 on NASDAQ and over 820 on NYSE ARCA). A significant advantage is that ETFs can be bought and sold (including short sales) continuously on an exchange like common stock. Although they do not have management fees, they do have expense fees, and there is the typical transaction cost for the purchase or sale of ETF shares.2 3.2.4 Special Equity Instruments: Options In addition to common stock investments, it is also possible to invest in equity-derivative securities, which are securities that have a claim on the common stock of a firm. This would include options—rights to buy or sell common stock at a specified price for a stated period of time. The two kinds of option instruments are: (1) warrants and (2) puts and calls. Warrants As mentioned earlier, a warrant is an option issued by a corporation that gives the holder the right to acquire a firm's common stock from the company at a specified price within a designated time period. The warrant does not constitute ownership of the stock, only the option to buy the stock. Puts and Calls A call option is similar to a warrant because it is an option to buy the common stock of a company within a certain period at a specified price called the striking price. A call option differs from a warrant because it is not issued by the company but by another investor who is willing to assume the other side of the transaction. Options also are typically valid for a shorter time period than warrants. Call options are generally valid for less than a year, whereas warrants often extend more than five years. The holder of a put option has the right to sell a given stock at a specified price during a designated time period. Puts are useful to investors who expect a stock price to decline during the specified period or to investors who own the stock and want hedge protection from a price decline. 3.2.5 Futures Contracts Another instrument that provides an alternative to the purchase of an investment is a futures contract. This agreement provides for the future exchange of a particular asset at a specified delivery date (usually within nine months) in exchange for a specified payment at the time of delivery. Although the full payment is not made until the delivery date, a good-faith deposit, the margin, is made to protect the seller. This is typically about 10 percent of the value of the contract. The bulk of trading on the commodity exchanges is in futures contracts. The current price of the futures contract is determined by the participants' beliefs about the future for the commodity. For example, in July of a given year, a trader could speculate on the Chicago Board of 2 Mutual funds and ETFs are discussed further in the next section and in Chapters 16 and 25. 78 Part 1: The Investment Background WWW.YAZDANPRESS.COM Trade for wheat in September, December, March, and May of the next year. If the investor expected the price of a commodity to rise, he or she could buy a futures contract on one of the commodity exchanges for later sale. If the investor expected the price to fall, he or she could sell a futures contract on an exchange with the expectation of buying similar contracts later when the price had (hopefully) declined to cover the sale. Several differences exist between investing in an asset through a futures contract and investing in the asset itself. One is the use of a small good-faith deposit, which increases the volatility of returns. Because an investor puts up only a small portion of the total value of the futures contract (10 to 15 percent), when the price of the commodity changes, the change in the total value of the contract (up or down) is large compared to the amount invested. Another unique aspect is the term of the investment: Although stocks can have infinite maturities, futures contracts typically expire in less than a year. Financial Futures In addition to futures contracts on commodities, there also has been the development of futures contracts on financial instruments, such as T-bills, Treasury bonds, and Eurobonds. For example, it is possible to buy or sell a futures contract that promises future delivery of $100,000 of Treasury bonds at a set price and yield. The major exchanges for financial futures are the Chicago Mercantile Exchange (CME) and the Chicago Board of Trade (CBOT).3 These futures contracts allow individual investors, bond portfolio managers, and corporate financial managers to protect themselves against volatile interest rates. Certain currency futures allow individual investors or portfolio managers to speculate on or to protect against changes in currency exchange rates. Finally, there are futures contracts on various stock market series, such as the S&P (Standard & Poor's) 500, the Value

Line Index, and the Nikkei Average on the Tokyo Stock Exchange. 3.2.6 Investment Companies The investment alternatives described so far are individual securities that can be acquired from a government entity, a corporation, or another individual. However, rather than directly buying an individual stock or bond issued by one of these sources, you may choose to acquire these investments indirectly by buying shares in an investment company that owns a portfolio of individual stocks, bonds, or a combination of the two. Specifically, an investment company sells shares in itself and invests the pooled investor dollars in bonds, stocks, or other investment instruments. The main types of investment companies are mutual funds, closed-end funds, and exchange-traded funds. Mutual funds are also referred to as open-ended funds because they issue "redeemable securities" meaning that the fund stands ready to buy or sell the shares at their net asset value with (a load) or without (no-load) a transaction fee. A closedend fund issues a fixed number of shares that trade intraday on stock exchanges at marketdetermined prices. Investors in a closed-end fund buy or sell shares through a broker just like any publicly traded company. An exchange traded fund (ETF) is an investment company, typically a mutual fund whose shares are traded intraday on stock exchanges at marketdetermined prices—in contrast to open-ended funds that are priced only once a day at the market closing prices. Investors may buy or sell ETF shares through a broker just as they would the shares of any publicly traded company. An investor who acquires shares in an investment company is a partial owner of the investment company's portfolio of stocks or bonds. In the following discussion we will distinguish between investment companies by the types of investment instruments they acquire. Money Market Funds Money market funds are investment companies that acquire highquality, short-term investments (referred to as money market instruments), such as T-bills, 3 These two exchanges merged in early 2008. Chapter 3: Selecting Investments in a Global Market 79 WWW.YAZDANPRESS.COM high-grade commercial paper (public short-term loans) from various corporations, and large CDs from the major money center banks. The yields on the money market portfolios always surpass those on normal bank CDs because the investment by the money market fund is larger and the fund can commit to longer maturities than the typical individual. In addition, the returns on commercial paper are above the prime rate. The typical minimum initial investment in a money market fund is $1,000, it charges no sales commission, and minimum additions are $250 to $500. You can always withdraw funds from your money market fund without penalty (typically by writing a check on the account), and you receive interest to the day of withdrawal. Individuals tend to use money market funds as alternatives to bank savings accounts because they are generally quite safe (although they are not insured, they typically limit their investments to high-quality, short-term investments), they provide yields above what is available on most savings accounts, and the funds are readily available. Therefore, you might use one of these funds to accumulate funds to pay tuition or for a down payment on a car. Because of relatively high yields and extreme flexibility and liquidity, the total value of these funds reached almost $4 trillion in 2011. Bond Funds Bond funds generally invest in various long-term government, corporate, or municipal bonds. They differ by the type and quality of the bonds included in the portfolio as assessed by various rating services. Specifically, the bond funds range from those that invest only in risk-free government bonds and high-grade corporate bonds to those that concentrate in lower-rated corporate or municipal bonds, called high-yield bonds or junk bonds. The expected yields from various bond funds will differ, with the low-risk government bond funds paying the lowest yields and the high-yield bond funds expected to provide the highest yields. Common Stock Funds Numerous common stock funds invest to achieve stated investment objectives, which can include aggressive growth, income, precious metal investments, and international stocks. Such funds offer smaller investors the benefits of diversification and professional management. They include different investment styles, such as growth or value, and concentrate in alternative-sized firms, including small-cap, mid-cap, and large-capitalization stocks. To meet the diverse needs of investors, numerous funds have been created that concentrate in one industry or sector of the economy, such as chemicals, electric utilities, health, housing, and technology. These funds are diversified within a sector or an industry, but are not diversified across the total market. Investors who participate in a sector or an industry fund bear more risk than investors in a total market fund because the sector funds will tend to fluctuate more than an aggregate market fund that is diversified across all sectors. Also, international funds that invest outside the United States and global funds that invest in the United States and in other countries offer opportunities for global diversification by individual investors, as documented by Bailey and Lim (1992). Balanced Funds Balanced funds invest in a combination of bonds and stocks of various sorts depending on their stated objectives. Index

Funds Index funds are mutual funds created to equal (track) the performance of a market index like the S&P 500. Such funds appeal to passive investors who want to simply experience returns equal to some market index either because they do not want to try to "beat the market" or they believe in efficient markets and do not think it is possible to do better than the market in the long run. Given the popularity of these funds, they have been created to emulate numerous stock indexes including very broad indexes like the Dow Jones Wilshire 5000 and broad foreign indexes like the EAFE index. In addition, numerous nonstock indexes including various bond indexes have been created for those who want passive bond investing.

Exchange-Traded Funds (ETFs) A problem with open-ended mutual funds in general and index funds in particular is that they are only priced daily at the close of the market and all transactions take place at that price. As a result, if you are aware of changes taking place for the aggregate market due to some economic event during the day and want to buy or sell to take advantage of this, you can put in an order for a mutual fund, but it will not be executed until the end of the day at closing prices. In response to this problem, the AMEX in 1993 created an indexed fund tied to the S&P 500—that is, an exchange-traded fund, ETF—that could be traded continuously because the prices for the 500 stocks are updated continuously so it is possible to buy and sell this ETF like a share of stock, as noted previously. As discussed earlier in the section on buying foreign securities, ETFs have been created for numerous foreign and domestic indexes including the Morgan Stanley Capital International (MSCI) indexes. Barclay's Global Investors (BGI) have created "i shares," using the MSCI indexes for numerous individual countries. The performance of these ETFs have been analyzed by Khorana, Nelling, and Trester (1998). As noted earlier, the growth in the number and value of ETFs over the past decade has been substantial. 3.2.7 Real Estate Like commodities, most investors view real estate as an interesting and profitable investment alternative but believe that it is only available to a small group of experts with a lot of capital to invest. In reality, some feasible real estate investments require no detailed expertise or large capital commitments. We will begin by considering low-capital alternatives. Real Estate Investment Trusts (REITS) A real estate investment trust is an investment fund designed to invest in various real estate properties. It is similar to a stock or bond mutual fund, except that the money provided by the investors is invested in property and buildings rather than in stocks and bonds. There are several types of REITs.

Construction and development trusts lend the money required by builders during the initial construction of a building. Mortgage trusts provide the long-term financing for properties. Specifically, they acquire long-term mortgages on properties once construction is completed. Equity trusts own various income-producing properties, such as office buildings, shopping centers, or apartment houses. Therefore, an investor who buys shares in an equity real estate investment trust is buying part of a portfolio of income-producing properties. REITs have experienced periods of great popularity and significant depression in line with changes in the aggregate economy and the money market. Although they are subject to cyclical risks depending on the economic environment, they offer small investors a way to participate in real estate investments, as described by Hardy (1995), Kuhn (1996), and Myer and Webb (1993). Direct Real Estate Investment The most common type of direct real estate investment is the purchase of a home, which is the largest investment most people ever make. According to the Federal Home Loan Bank, the average cost of a single family house in early 2011 exceeds $155,000. The purchase of a home is considered an investment because the buyer pays a sum of money either all at once or over a number of years through a mortgage. For most people who are unable to pay cash for a house, the financial commitment includes a down payment (typically 10–20 percent of the purchase price) and specific mortgage payments over a 20- to 30-year period that amortize both the loan's principal and interest due on the outstanding balance. Subsequently, a homeowner hopes to sell the house for its cost plus a gain. Raw Land Another direct real estate investment is the purchase of raw land with the intention of selling it in the future at a profit. During the time you own the land, you have negative cash flows caused by mortgage payments, property maintenance, and taxes. An obvious risk is Chapter 3: Selecting Investments in a Global Market 81 WWW.YAZDANPRESS.COM the possible difficulty of selling it for an uncertain price. Raw land generally has low liquidity compared to most stocks and bonds. An alternative to buying and selling the raw land is the development of the land. Land Development Land development can involve buying raw land, dividing it into individual lots, and building houses on it. Alternatively, buying land and building a shopping mall would also be considered land development. This is a feasible form of investment but requires a substantial commitment of capital, time, and expertise. Although the risks can be high because of the commitment of time and capital, the rates of return from a successful housing or commercial development can be significant, as shown in studies by Goetzmann and Ibbotson (1990) and Ross and Zisler (1991). Diversification benefits are documented in Hudson-Wilson and Elbaum (1995). Rental Property Many investors with an interest in real estate investing acquire apartment buildings or houses with low down payments, with the intention of deriving enough income from the rents to pay the expenses of the structure, including the mortgage payments. For the first few years following the purchase, the investor generally has no reported income from the building because of tax-deductible expenses, including the interest component of the mortgage payment and depreciation on the structure. Subsequently, rental property provides a cash flow and an opportunity to profit from the sale of the property, as discussed by Harris (1984). 3.2.8 Low-Liquidity Investments Most of the investment alternatives we have described thus far are traded on securities markets and except for real estate, have good liquidity. In contrast, the investments we discuss in this section have very poor liquidity and financial institutions do not typically acquire them because of the illiquidity and high transaction costs compared to stocks and bonds. Many of these assets are sold at auctions, causing expected prices to vary substantially. In addition, transaction costs are high because there is generally no national market for these investments, so local dealers must be compensated for the added carrying costs and the cost of searching for buyers or sellers. Therefore, many financial theorists view the following low-liquidity investments more as hobbies than investments, even though studies have indicated that some of these assets have experienced substantial rates of return. Antiques The greatest returns from antiques are earned by dealers who acquire them at estate sales or auctions to refurbish and sell at a profit. If we gauge the value of antiques based on prices established at large public auctions, it appears that many serious collectors enjoy substantial rates of return. In contrast, the average investor who owns a few pieces to decorate his or her home finds such returns elusive. The high transaction costs and illiquidity of antiques may erode any profit that the individual may expect to earn when selling these pieces. Art The entertainment sections of newspapers or the personal finance sections of magazines often carry stories of the results of major art auctions, such as when Van Gogh's Irises and Sunflowers sold for $59 million and $36 million, respectively. Obviously, these examples and others indicate that some paintings have increased significantly in value and thereby have generated large rates of return for their owners. However, investing in art typically requires substantial knowledge of art and the art world, a large amount of capital to acquire the work of well-known artists, patience, and an ability to absorb high transaction costs. For investors who enjoy fine art and have the resources, these can be satisfying investments; but, for most small investors, it is difficult to get returns that compensate for the uncertainty, illiquidity, and high transaction costs. 82 Part 1: The Investment Background WWW.YAZDANPRESS.COM Coins and Stamps Many individuals enjoy collecting coins or stamps as a hobby and as an investment. The market for coins and stamps is fragmented compared to the stock market, but it is more liquid than the market for art and antiques as indicated by the publication of weekly and monthly price lists.5 An investor can get a widely recognized grading specification on a coin or stamp, and, once graded, a coin or stamp can usually be sold quickly through a dealer, as described by Henriques (1989) and Bradford (1989). Notably, the percentage difference between the bid price the dealer will pay to buy the stamp or coin and the asking or selling price the investor must pay the dealer is going to be substantially larger than the bid-ask spread on stocks and bonds. Diamonds Diamonds can be and have been good investments during many periods. Still, investors who purchase diamonds must realize that (1) diamonds can be highly illiquid, (2) the grading process that determines their quality is quite subjective, (3) most investment-grade gems require substantial capital, and (4) they generate no positive cash flow during the holding period until the stone is sold. In fact, during the holding period, the investor must cover costs of insurance and storage and there are appraisal costs before selling. In this section, we have briefly described the most common investment alternatives. Following this brief description, we will discuss many of these investment alternatives in more detail when we consider how you evaluate them for investment purposes. In our final section, we present data on historical rates of return and risk measures, as well as correlations among several of these investments. This provides insights into future expected returns and risk characteristics (both total and systematic risk) for these investment alternatives. 3.3 HISTORICAL RISK-RETURNS ON ALTERNATIVE INVESTMENTS How do investors weigh the costs and benefits of owning investments and make decisions to build portfolios that will provide the best risk-return combinations? To help individual or institutional investors answer this question, financial theorists have examined extensive data to provide information on the return and risk characteristics of various investments. There have been numerous studies of the historical rates of return on common stocks (both large-capitalization stocks in terms of aggregate market value and small-capitalization stocks).6 In addition, there has been a growing interest in the performance of bonds. Because inflation has been so pervasive, many studies include both nominal and real rates of return on investments. Still other investigators have examined the performance of alternative assets such as real estate, foreign stocks, art, antiques, and commodities. The review of these results should help you to make decisions on building your investment portfolio and on the allocation to the various asset classes. 3.3.1 World Portfolio Performance A study by Reilly and Wright (2004) examined the performance of numerous assets, not only in the United States, but around the world. Specifically, for the period from 1980 to 2001, they 5 A weekly publication for coins is Coin World, published by Amos Press, Inc., 911 Vandermark Rd., Sidney, OH 45367. There are several monthly coin magazines, including Coinage, published by Miller Magazines, Ventura, CA. Amos Press also publishes several stamp magazines, including Linn's Stamp News and Scott Stamp Monthly. These magazines provide current prices for coins and stamps. 6 Small-capitalization stocks were broken out as a separate class of asset because several studies have shown that firms with relatively small capitalization (stock with low market value) have experienced rates of return and risk significantly different from those of stocks in general. Therefore, they were considered a unique asset class. We will discuss these studies in Chapter 6, which deals with the efficient markets hypothesis. The large-company stock returns are based upon the S&P Composite Index of 500 stocks—the S&P 500 (examined the performance of stocks, bonds, cash (the equivalent of U.S. T-bills), real estate, and commodities from the world, United States, Europe, Pacific Basin, Japan, and the emerging markets. They computed annual returns, risk measures, and correlations among the returns for alternative assets. Exhibit 3.8 contains updated geometric and arithmetic average annual rates of return, the standard deviations of returns, and the systematic risk (beta) for modified set of series for the 31-year period 1980–2010 (the authors deleted and added several series due to availability of the data). Asset Return and Total Risk The results in Exhibit 3.8 generally confirm the expected relationship between annual rates of return and the total risk (standard deviation) of these securities. The riskier assets with higher standard deviations experienced higher returns. For example, the U.S. stock indexes had relatively high returns (10 to 17 percent) and large standard deviations (15 to 23 percent). It is not a surprise that the highest-risk asset class (without commodities) was the two emerging market stock indexes with standard deviations of 22.98 and 24.92 percent, whereas risk-free U.S. cash equivalents (30-day T-bills) had low returns (4.96 percent) and the smallest standard deviation (0.90 percent). Return and Systematic Risk As shown in Exhibit 3.8, in addition to total risk (standard deviation), the authors also considered systematic risk, which is the volatility of an asset relative to a market portfolio of risky assets (this was discussed briefly in Chapter 1). One of the conclusions of the Reilly and Wright (2004) study was that the systematic risk measure (beta) did a better job of explaining the returns during the period than the total risk measure (standard deviation). In addition, the systematic risk measure (beta) that used the Brinson Global Security Market Index (GSMI) as a market proxy was somewhat better than the beta that used the S&P 500 Index.7 Thus, Exhibit 3.9, which contains the scatter plot of geometric mean rate of return and GSMI systematic risk, indicates the expected positive risk–return relationship. The two outliers are the Tokyo Stock Exchange Index on the low side and the Wilshire 5000 equal-weighted index. Correlations between Asset Returns Exhibit 3.10 contains a correlation matrix of selected U.S. and world assets. The first column shows that U.S. equities (as represented by the broad Wilshire 5000 Index) have a reasonably high correlation with most developed countries but low correlation with emerging market stocks and Pacific Basin stocks. Also, U.S. equities show almost zero correlation with world government bonds, and with the commodities index. Recall from our earlier discussion that you can use this information to build a diversified portfolio by combining those assets with low positive or negative correlations.The correlation of returns with inflation has implications regarding the ability of an asset class to be an inflation hedge—a good inflation hedge should have a strong positive correlation with inflation. As shown, most assets (including common stocks) have negative correlations with inflation, which implies that they are poor inflation hedges. The exceptions appear to be commodities (0.20) and short-term government bonds (especially 30-day Treasury bills with 0.41 correlation). 3.3.2 Art and Antiques Unlike financial securities, where the results of transactions are reported daily, art and antique markets are fragmented and lack any formal transaction reporting system. This makes it difficult to gather data. The best-known series that attempted to provide information about the changing value of art and antiques were developed by Sotheby's, a major art auction firm. These value indexes covered 13 areas of art and antiques and a weighted aggregate series that combined the 13 areas. Reilly (1992) examined these series for the period from 1976 to 1991 and computed rates of return, measures of risk, and the correlations among the various art and antique series and compared them to stocks, bonds, and the rate of inflation. Although there was a wide range of mean returns and risk, a risk-return plot indicated a fairly consistent relationship between risk and return during this 16 year period. Comparing the art and antique results to bond and stock indexes indicated that stocks and bonds experienced results that were very consistent with the art and antique series. Analysis of the correlations among these assets using annual rates of return revealed several important relationships. First, the correlations among alternative antique and art categories vary substantially from above 0.90 to negative correlations. Second, the correlations between art/antiques and bonds were generally negative. Third, the correlations of art/antiques with stocks were typically small positive values. Finally, the correlation of art and antiques with the rate of inflation indicates that several of the categories were fairly good inflation hedges since they were positively correlated with inflation. Notably, they were clearly superior inflation hedges compared to long-term bonds and common stocks as documented in Fama (1991) and Jaffe and Mandelker (1976). The reader should recall our earlier observation that most art and antiques are quite illiquid and the transaction costs are fairly high compared to financial assets.8 3.3.3 Real Estate Somewhat similar to art and antiques, returns on real estate are difficult to derive because of the limited number of transactions and the lack of a national source of data for the transactions that allows one to accurately compute rates of return. In the study by Goetzmann and Ibbotson (1990), the authors gathered data on commercial real estate through REITs and Commingled Real Estate Funds (CREFs) and estimated returns on residential real estate from a series created by Case and Shiller (1987). The summary of the real estate returns compared to various stock, bond, and an inflation series is contained in Exhibit 3.11. As shown, the two commercial real estate series reflected strikingly different results. The CREFs had lower returns and low volatility, while the REIT index had higher returns and risk. Notably, the REIT returns were higher than those of common stocks, but the risk measure for real estate was lower (there was a small difference in the time period). The residential real estate series reflected lower returns and low risk. The longer-term results indicate that all the real estate series experienced lower returns and much lower risk than common stock. The correlations in Exhibit 3.12 among annual returns for the various asset groups indicate a relatively low positive correlation between commercial real estate and stocks. In contrast, there was negative correlation between stocks and residential and farm real estate. This negative relationship with real estate was also true for 20-year government bonds. Studies by Eichholtz (1996), Mull and Socnen (1997), and Quan and Titman (1997) that considered international commercial real estate and REITs indicated that the returns were correlated with stock prices but they still provided significant diversification benefits. These results imply that returns on real estate are equal to or slightly lower than returns on common stocks, but real estate possesses favorable risk and diversification results. Specifically individual real estate assets had much lower standard deviations and either low positive or negative correlations with other asset classes in a portfolio context. Finally, all the real estate series had significant positive correlation with inflation, which implies strong potential as an inflation hedge.

CHAPTER FIVE

Organization and Functioning of Securities Markets

The stock market, the Dow Jones Industrials, and the bond market are part of our everyday experience. Each evening on television news broadcasts we find out how stocks and bonds fared; each morning we read in our daily newspapers about expectations for a market rally or decline. Yet most people have an imperfect understanding of how domestic and world capital markets actually function. To be a successful investor in a global environment, you must know what financial markets are available around the world and how they operate. In this chapter, we take a broad view of securities markets and provide a detailed discussion of how major stock markets function. We also consider how global securities markets have been changing during recent years and discuss how they will probably change in the future. We begin with a discussion of securities markets and the characteristics of a good market. We describe two components of the capital markets: primary and secondary. Our main emphasis is on the secondary stock market including the national stock exchanges around the world and how these markets, separated by geography and by time zones, are becoming linked into a 24-hour market. We also consider a detailed analysis of how alternative exchange markets operate, including the Electronic Communication Networks (ECNs). In the final section, we consider numerous recent changes in financial markets, including significant mergers, and future changes expected. These numerous changes in our securities markets will have a profound effect on what investments are available from around the world, how we buy and sell them, and at what cost. 4.1 WHAT IS A MARKET? A market is the means through which buyers and sellers are brought together to aid in the transfer of goods and/or services. Several aspects of this general definition seem worthy of emphasis. First, a market need not have a physical location. It is only necessary that the buyers and sellers can communicate regarding the relevant aspects of the transaction. Second, the market does not necessarily own the goods or services involved. The important criterion for a good market is the smooth, cheap transfer of goods and services. Those who establish and administer the market do not own the assets but simply provide a system that allows potential buyers and sellers to interact. They help the market function by providing information and facilities to aid in the transfer of ownership. Finally, a market can deal in any variety of goods and services. For any commodity or service with a diverse clientele, a market should evolve to aid in the transfer of that commodity or service. Both buyers and sellers benefit from the existence of a market. 4.1.1 Characteristics of a Good Market Throughout this book, we will discuss markets for different investments such as stocks, bonds, options, and futures in the United States and throughout the world. We will refer to these markets using various terms of quality such as strong, active, liquid, or illiquid. There are many financial markets, but they are not all equal—some are active and liquid, others are relatively illiquid and inefficient in their operations. To appreciate these discussions, you should be aware of the following characteristics that investors look for when evaluating the quality of a market. One enters a market to buy or sell a good or service quickly at a price justified by the prevailing supply and demand. To determine the appropriate price, participants must have timely and accurate information on the volume and prices of past transactions and all currently outstanding bids and offers. Therefore, one attribute of a good market is timely and accurate information on past transactions and prevailing buy and sell orders. Another prime requirement is liquidity, the ability to buy or sell an asset quickly and at a known price—that is, a price not substantially different from the prices for prior transactions, assuming no new information is available. An asset's likelihood of being sold quickly, sometimes referred to as its marketability, is a necessary, but not a sufficient, condition for liquidity. The expected price should also be fairly certain, based on the recent history of transaction prices and current bid-ask quotes. For a formal discussion of liquidity, see Handa and Schwartz (1996) and AIMR's articles on Best Execution and Portfolio Performance (Jost, 2001). A component of liquidity is price continuity, which means that prices do not change much from one transaction to the next unless substantial new information becomes available. Suppose no new information is forthcoming, and the last transaction was at a price of $20; if the next trade were at between $19.95 and $20.05, the market would be considered reasonably 96 Part 1: The Investment Background WWW.YAZDANPRESS.COM continuous.1 A continuous market without large price changes between trades is a characteristic of a liquid market. A market with price continuity requires depth, which means that there are numerous potential buyers and sellers willing to trade at prices above and below the current market price. These buyers and sellers enter the market in response to changes in supply, demand, or both, and thereby prevent drastic price changes. In summary, liquidity requires marketability and price continuity, which, in turn, requires depth. Another factor contributing to a good market is the transaction cost. Lower costs (as a percent of the value of the trade) make for a more efficient market. An individual comparing the cost of a transaction between markets would choose a market that charges 2 percent of the value of the trade compared with one that charges 5 percent. Most microeconomic textbooks define an efficient market as one in which the cost of the transaction is minimal. This attribute is referred to as internal efficiency. 2 Finally, a buyer or seller wants the prevailing market price to adequately reflect all the information available regarding supply and demand factors in the market. If such conditions change as a result of new information, the price should change accordingly. Therefore, participants want prices to adjust quickly to new information regarding supply or demand, which means that prevailing market prices reflect all available information about the asset. This attribute is referred to as external, or informational, efficiency. We discuss this attribute extensively in Chapter 6. In summary, a good market for goods and services has the following characteristics: 1. Timely and accurate information on the price and volume of past transactions. 2. Liquidity, meaning an asset can be bought or sold quickly at a price close to the prices for previous transactions (has price continuity), assuming no new information has been received. In turn, price continuity requires depth. 3. Low transaction costs, including the cost of reaching the market, the actual brokerage costs, and the cost of transferring the asset. 4. Prices that rapidly adjust to new information, so the prevailing price is fair since it reflects all available information regarding the asset. 4.1.2 Decimal Pricing Prior to the initiation of changes in late 2000 that were completed in early 2001, common stocks in the United States were always quoted in fractions. Specifically, prior to 1997 they were quoted in eighths (e.g., 1 8; 2 8;:: :;

7 8), with each eighth equal to $0.125. This was modified in 1997 when the fractions for most stocks went to sixteenths (e.g., 1 16; 2 16;:: :; 15 16) equal to $0.0625. Now U.S. equities are priced in decimals (cents), so the minimum spread can be in cents (e.g., $30.10–$30.12). The espoused reasons for the change to decimal pricing are threefold. First, is the ease with which investors can understand and compare prices. Second, decimal pricing reduces the size of the bid-ask spread from a minimum of 6.25 cents (when prices are quoted in sixteenths) to 1 cent (when prices are in decimals). Many brokers and investment firms were against the change since the spread is the price of liquidity for the investor and the compensation to the dealer. Third, the change made U.S. markets more competitive on a global basis since other countries were pricing on a comparable basis. 1 You should be aware that common stocks are currently sold in decimals (dollars and cents), which is a change from the pre-2000 period when stocks were priced in eighths and sixteenths. This change to decimals is discussed in the following subsection. 2 A subsequent discussion in this chapter on new innovations will make it clear that new technology and competition has resulted in a very internally efficient global equity market. Chapter 4: Organization and Functioning of Securities Markets 97 WWW.YAZDANPRESS.COM Decimalization has reduced spread size and transaction costs, which has led to a decline in transaction size and an increase in the number of transactions. For example, the number of transactions on the NYSE went from a daily average of 877,000 in 2000 to over 10 million during 2010, while the average trade size went from 1,187 shares in 2000 to about 300 shares in 2010. 4.1.3 Organization of the Securities Market Before we discuss the specific operation of the securities market, we need to understand its overall organization. The principal distinction is between primary markets, where new securities are sold, and secondary markets, where outstanding securities are bought and sold. Each of these markets is further divided based on the economic unit that issued the security. We will consider each of these major segments of the securities market, with an emphasis on the individuals involved and the functions they perform. 4.2 PRIMARY CAPITAL MARKETS The primary market is where new issues of bonds, preferred stock, or common stock are sold by government units, municipalities, or companies who want to acquire new capital. For a review of studies on the primary market, see Jensen and Smith (1986). 4.2.1 Government Bond Issues U.S. government bond issues are subdivided into three segments based on their original maturities.

Treasury bills are negotiable, non-interest-bearing securities with original maturities of one year or less. Treasury notes have original maturities of 2 to 10 years. Finally, Treasury bonds have original maturities of more than 10 years. To sell bills, notes, and bonds, the Treasury relies on Federal Reserve System auctions. (The bidding process and pricing are discussed in Chapter 17.) 4.2.2 Municipal Bond Issues New municipal bond issues are sold by one of three methods: competitive bid, negotiation, or private placement. Competitive bid sales typically involve sealed bids. The bond issue is sold to the bidding syndicate of underwriters that submits the bid with the lowest interest cost in accordance with the stipulations set forth by the issuer. Negotiated sales involve contractual arrangements between underwriters and issuers wherein the underwriter helps the issuer prepare the bond issue and set the price and has the exclusive right to sell the issue. Private placements involve the sale of a bond issue by the issuer directly to an investor or a small group of investors (usually institutions). Note that two of the three methods require an underwriting function. Specifically, in a competitive bid or a negotiated transaction, the investment banker typically underwrites the issue, which means the investment firm purchases the entire issue at a specified price, relieving the issuer from the risk and responsibility of selling and distributing the bonds. Subsequently, the underwriter sells the issue to the investing public. For municipal bonds, this underwriting function is performed by both investment banking firms and commercial banks. The underwriting function can involve three services: origination, risk-bearing, and distribution. Origination involves the design of the bond issue and initial planning. To fulfill the riskbearing function, the underwriter acquires the total issue at a price dictated by the competitive bid or through negotiation and accepts the responsibility and risk of reselling it for more than the purchase price. Distribution means selling it to investors, typically with the help of a selling syndicate that includes other investment banking firms and/or commercial banks. 98 Part 1: The Investment Background WWW.YAZDANPRESS.COM In a negotiated bid, the underwriter will carry out all three services. In a competitive bid, the issuer specifies the amount, maturities, coupons, and call features of the issue and the competing syndicates submit a bid for the entire issue that reflects the yields they estimate for the bonds. The issuer may have received advice from an investment firm on the desirable characteristics for a forthcoming issue, but this advice would have been on a fee basis and would not necessarily involve the ultimate underwriter who is responsible for risk-bearing and distribution. Finally, a private placement involves no risk-bearing, but an investment banker would typically assist in designing the characteristics of the issue and locating potential buyers. 4.2.3 Corporate Bond Issues Corporate bond issues are almost always sold through a negotiated arrangement with an investment banking firm that maintains a relationship with the issuing firm. In a global capital market there has been an explosion of new instruments, which means that the origination function, which involves designing the characteristics and currency for the security, is becoming more important because the corporate chief financial officer (CFO) may not be completely familiar with the availability and issuing requirements of many new instruments and the alternative capital markets around the world. Investment banking firms compete for underwriting business by creating new instruments that appeal to existing investors and by advising issuers regarding desirable countries and currencies. As a result, the expertise of the investment banker can help reduce the issuer's cost of new capital. Once a stock or bond issue is specified, the underwriter will put together an underwriting syndicate of other major underwriters and a selling group of smaller firms for its distribution, as shown in Exhibit 4.1. 4.2.4 Corporate Stock Issues In addition to issuing fixed-income securities, corporations can also issue equity securities— generally common stock. For corporations, new stock issues are typically divided into two groups: (1) seasoned equity issues, and (2) initial public offerings (IPOs). Exhibit 4.1 The Underwriting Organization Structure Underwriting Group Selling Group Issuing Firm Investment Banker A Investment Banker B Investment Banker C Investors Institutions Individuals Investment Firm A Investment Firm B Investment Firm C Investment Firm D Investment Firm E Investment Firm F Investment Firm G Investment Banker D Lead Underwriter Chapter 4: Organization and Functioning of Securities Markets 99 WWW.YAZDANPRESS.COM Seasoned equity issues are new shares offered by firms that already have stock outstanding. An example would be General Electric, which is a large, well-regarded firm that has had public stock trading on the NYSE for longer than 50 years. If General Electric needed additional capital, it could sell additional shares of its common stock to the public at a price very close to the current market price of the firm's stock. Initial public offerings (IPOs) involve a firm selling its common stock to the public for the first time. At the time of an IPO, there is no existing public market for the stock; that is, the company has been closely held. An example was an IPO by Polo Ralph Lauren, a leading manufacturer and distributor of men's clothing. The purpose of the offering was to get additional capital to expand its operations and to create a public market for future seasonal offerings. New issues (seasoned or IPOs) are typically underwritten by investment bankers, who acquire the total issue from the company and sell the securities to interested investors. The lead underwriter gives advice to the corporation on the general characteristics of the issue, its pricing, the timing of the offering, and participates in a "road show" visiting potential institutional investors. The underwriter also accepts the risk of selling the new issue after acquiring it from the corporation. For further discussion, see Brealey and Myers (2010, Chapter 15). Relationships with Investment Bankers The underwriting of corporate issues typically takes one of three forms: negotiated, competitive bids, or best-efforts arrangements. As noted, negotiated underwritings are the most common, and the procedure is the same as for municipal issues. A corporation may also specify the type of securities to be offered (common stock, preferred stock, or bonds) and then solicit competitive bids from investment banking firms. This is rare for industrial firms but is typical for utilities, which may be required by law to sell the issue via a competitive bid. Although a competitive bid typically reduces the cost of an issue, it also means that the investment banker gives less advice but still accepts the risk-bearing function by underwriting the issue and fulfills the distribution function. Alternatively, an investment banker can agree to sell an issue on a best-efforts basis. This is usually done with speculative new issues. In this arrangement, the investment banker does not underwrite the issue because it does not buy any securities. The stock is owned by the company, and the investment banker acts as a broker to sell whatever it can at a stipulated price. Because it bears no risk, the investment banker earns a lower commission on such an issue than on an underwritten issue. Introduction of Rule 415 The typical practice of negotiated arrangements involving numerous investment banking firms in syndicates and selling groups has changed with the introduction of Rule 415, which allows large firms to register security issues and sell them piecemeal during the following two years. These issues are referred to as shelf registrations because, after they are registered, the issues lie on the shelf and can be taken down and sold on short notice whenever it suits the issuing firm. As an example, Apple Computer could register an issue of 5 million shares of common stock during 2012 and sell a million shares in early 2012, another million shares in late 2012, 2 million shares in early 2013, and the rest in late 2013. Each offering can be made with little notice or paperwork by one underwriter or several. In fact, because relatively few shares may be involved, the lead underwriter often handles the whole deal without a syndicate or uses only one or two other firms. This arrangement has benefited large corporations because it provides great flexibility, reduces registration fees and expenses, and allows issuing firms to request competitive bids from several investment banking firms. On the other hand, some observers fear that shelf registrations do not allow investors enough time to examine the current status of the firm issuing the securities. Also, the follow-up offerings reduce the participation of small underwriters. Shelf registrations have typically been used for the sale of straight debentures rather than common stock or convertible issues. For further discussion of Rule 415, see Rogowski and Sorensen (1985). 100 Part 1: The Investment Background WWW.YAZDANPRESS.COM 4.2.5 Private Placements and Rule 144A Rather than a public sale using one of these arrangements, primary offerings can be sold privately. In such an arrangement, referred to as a private placement, the firm designs an issue with the assistance of an investment banker and sells it to a small group of institutions. The firm enjoys lower issuing costs because it does not need to prepare the extensive registration statement required for a public offering. Institutions buying the issue typically benefit because the issuing firm passes some of the cost savings on to the investor as a higher return. In fact, pre-Rule 144A an institution required a higher return because of the absence of any secondary market for these securities, which implied higher liquidity risk. The private placement market changed dramatically when Rule 144A was introduced by the SEC. This rule allows corporations—including non-U.S. firms—to place securities privately with large, sophisticated institutional investors without extensive registration documents. A major innovation is that these securities can subsequently be traded among these large sophisticated investors (those with assets in excess of $100 million). The SEC introduced this innovation to provide more financing alternatives for U.S. and non-U.S. firms and possibly increase the number, size, and liquidity of private placements, as discussed by Milligan (1990) and Hanks (1990). Presently, more than 85 percent of high-yield bonds are 144A issues. 4.3 SECONDARY FINANCIAL MARKETS In this section, we consider the importance of secondary markets and provide an overview of the secondary markets for bonds, financial futures, and stocks. Next, we consider national stock markets around the world.

Finally, we discuss other primary listing markets, regional exchanges, third markets, and the rapidly growing electronic communication networks (ECNs) and alternative trading systems (ATSs) and provide a detailed presentation on the functioning of stock exchanges. Secondary markets permit trading in outstanding issues; that is, stocks or bonds already sold to the public are traded between current and potential owners. The proceeds from a sale in the secondary market do not go to the issuing unit (the government, municipality, or company), but rather to the current owner of the security. 4.3.1 Why Secondary Markets Are Important Because the secondary market involves the trading of securities initially sold in the primary market, it provides liquidity to the individuals who acquired these securities. The point is, after acquiring securities in the primary market, investors may want to sell them again to acquire other securities, buy a house, or go on a vacation. The primary market benefits from this liquidity because investors would hesitate to acquire securities in the primary market if they thought they could not subsequently sell them in the secondary market. That is, without an active secondary market, potential issuers of stocks or bonds in the primary market would have to provide a much higher rate of return to compensate investors for the substantial liquidity risk. Secondary markets are also important to those selling seasoned securities because the prevailing market price of the securities (price discovery) is determined by transactions in the secondary market. New issues of outstanding stocks or bonds to be sold in the primary market are based on prices and yields in the secondary market. Notably, the secondary market also affects market efficiency and price volatility, as discussed by Foster and Viswanathan (1993) and Jones, Kaul, and Lipson (1994). Even forthcoming IPOs are priced based on the prices and values of comparable stocks or bonds in the public secondary market. Chapter 4: Organization and Functioning of Securities Markets 101 WWW.YAZDANPRESS.COM 4.3.2 Secondary Bond Markets The secondary market for bonds distinguishes among those issued by the federal government, municipalities, or corporations. Secondary Markets for U.S. Government and Municipal Bonds U.S. government bonds are traded by bond dealers that specialize in either Treasury bonds or agency bonds. Treasury issues are bought or sold through a set of 35 primary dealers, including large banks in New York and Chicago and some large investment banking firms like Goldman Sachs and Morgan Stanley. These institutions and other firms also make markets for government agency issues, but there is no formal set of dealers for agency securities. The major market makers in the secondary municipal bond market are banks and investment firms. Banks are active in municipal bond trading and underwriting of general obligation issues since they invest heavily in these securities. Also, many large investment firms have municipal bond departments that underwrite and trade these issues. Secondary Corporate Bond Markets Currently, all corporate bonds are traded over the counter by dealers who buy and sell for their own accounts. The major bond dealers are the large investment banking firms that underwrite the issues: firms such as Goldman Sachs, J.P. Morgan, Barclay Capital, and Morgan Stanley. Because of the limited trading in corporate bonds compared to the fairly active trading in government bonds, corporate bond dealers do not carry extensive inventories of specific issues. Instead, they hold a limited number of bonds desired by their clients, and when someone wants to do a trade, they work more like brokers than dealers. Notably, there is a movement toward a widespread transaction-reporting service as with stocks, especially for large, actively traded bond issues. As discussed in Chapter 17, starting in 2005, dealers have been required to report trades within 15 minutes for transactions on 17,000 corporate bonds. Exhibit 4.2 is a daily table from The Wall Street Journal that provides data for a large set of secondary bond indexes that are similar to various stock indexes. 4.3.3 Financial Futures In addition to the market for the bonds, a market has developed for futures contracts related to these bonds. These contracts allow the holder to buy or sell a specified amount of a given bond issue at a stipulated price. The two major futures exchanges are the Chicago Board of Trade (CBOT) and the Chicago Mercantile Exchange (CME) that merged during 2007. We discuss these futures contracts and the futures market in Chapter 19. 4.3.4 Secondary Equity Markets Before 2000, the secondary equity markets in the United States and around the world were divided into three segments: national stock exchanges, regional stock exchanges, and over-thecounter (OTC) markets for stocks not on an exchange. Because of numerous changes over the past decade, a better classification has been suggested by O'Hara and Ye (2011), as presented in Exhibit 4.3. Following our background discussions on alternative trading systems and call versus continuous markets, we will describe the market types listed in Exhibit 4.3 and discuss how they complement and compete against each other to provide price discovery and liquidity to individual and institutional investors.

CHAPTER SIX

Security-Market Indexes

A fair statement regarding security-market indexes—especially those outside the United States—is that everybody talks about them but few people understand them. Even those investors familiar with widely publicized stock-market series, such as the Dow Jones Industrial Average (DJIA), usually know little about indexes for the U.S. bond market or for non-U.S. stock markets such as Tokyo or London. Although portfolios are obviously composed of many different individual stocks, investors typically ask, "What happened to the market today?" The reason for this question is that if an investor owns more than a few stocks or bonds, it is cumbersome to follow each stock or bond individually to determine the composite performance of the portfolio. Also, there is an intuitive notion that most individual stocks or bonds move with the aggregate market. Therefore, if the overall market rose, an individual's portfolio probably also increased in value. To supply investors with a composite report on market performance, some financial publications or investment firms have created and maintain stock-market and bond-market indexes. In the initial section of this chapter, we discuss several ways that investors use security-market indexes. An awareness of these significant functions should provide an incentive for becoming familiar with these indexes and indicates why we present a full chapter on this topic. In the second section, we consider what characteristics cause various indexes to differ. Investors need to understand these differences and why one index is preferable for a given task because of its characteristics. In the third section, we present the most well-known U.S. and global stock-market indexes, separated into groups based on the weighting scheme used. In section four, we consider bond-market indexes that are becoming a more important topic because the bond 123 market continues to grow in size and importance for individuals and institutions.1 Again, we consider international bond indexes following the domestic indexes. In the fifth section, we consider composite stock market-bond market series. In our final section, we examine how alternative indexes relate to each other over monthly intervals. This comparison demonstrates the important factors that cause high or low correlation among series. With this background, you should be able to make an intelligent choice of the market index that is best for you based on how you want to use it. 5.1 USES OF SECURITY-MARKET INDEXES Security-market indexes have at least five significant uses. A primary application is to use the index values to compute total returns and risk measures for an aggregate market or some component of a market over a specified time period. In turn, many investors use the computed return-risk results as a benchmark to judge the performance of individual portfolios. A basic assumption when evaluating portfolio performance is that any investor should be able to experience a risk-adjusted rate of return comparable to the market by randomly selecting a large number of stocks or bonds from the total market; hence, a superior portfolio manager should consistently do better than the market. Therefore, an aggregate stock or bond-market index can be used as a benchmark to judge the performance of professional money managers. An obvious use of indexes is to develop an index portfolio. As we have discussed, it is difficult for most money managers to consistently outperform specified market indexes on a riskadjusted basis over time.2 If this is true, an obvious alternative is to invest in a portfolio that will emulate this market portfolio. This notion led to the creation of index funds and exchangetraded funds (ETFs), whose purpose is to track the performance of the specified market series (index) over time. The original index funds were common-stock funds as discussed in Malkiel (2007), Chapter 14, and Mossavar-Rahmani (2005). The development of comprehensive, wellspecified bond-market indexes and the inability of most bond-portfolio managers to outperform these indexes have led to a similar phenomenon in the fixed-income area (bond-index funds), as noted by Hawthorne (1986) and Dialynas (2001). Securities analysts, portfolio managers, and academicians doing research use securitymarket indexes to examine the factors that influence aggregate security price movements (that is, the indexes are used to measure aggregate market movements) and to compare the risk-adjusted performance of alternative asset classes (e.g., stocks versus bonds versus real estate). An extension of this is to examine the relative performance within asset classes such as large-cap stocks versus small-cap stocks. Another group interested in an aggregate market index is composed of "technicians," who believe past price changes can be used to predict future price movements. For example, to project future stock price movements, technicians would plot and analyze price and volume changes for a stock-market series like the Dow Jones Industrial Average or the S&P 500 index. Finally, work in portfolio and capital market theory has implied that the relevant risk for an individual risky asset is its systematic risk, which is the relationship between the rates of return for a risky asset and the rates of return for a market portfolio of risky assets.3 Therefore, an aggregate market index is used as a proxy for the market portfolio of risky assets. 1 This significant growth is well documented in Chapter 17. 2 Throughout this chapter and the book, we will use indicator series and indexes interchangeably, although indicator series is the more correct specification because it refers to a broad class of series; one popular type of series is an index, but there can be other types and many different indexes. 3 This concept and its justification are discussed in Chapter 7 and Chapter 8. Subsequently, in Chapter 25, we consider the difficulty of finding an index that is an appropriate proxy for the theoretical market portfolio of risky assets. 124 Part 1: The Investment Background WWW.YAZDANPRESS.COM 5.2 DIFFERENTIATING FACTORS IN CONSTRUCTING MARKET INDEXES Because the indexes are intended to reflect the overall movements of a group of securities, we need to consider three factors that are important when constructing an index intended to represent a total population. 5.2.1 The Sample The first factor is the sample used to construct an index. The size, the breadth, and the source of the sample are all important. A small percentage of the total population will provide valid indications of the behavior of the total population if the sample is properly selected. In some cases, because of the economics of computers, virtually all the stocks on an exchange or market are included, with a few deletions of unusual securities. Assuming you are not including the total population, the sample should be representative of the total population; otherwise, its size will be meaningless. A large biased sample is no better than a small biased sample. The sample can be generated by completely random selection or by a nonrandom selection technique designed to incorporate the important characteristics of the desired population. Finally, the source of the sample is important if there are any differences between segments of the population, in which case samples from each segment are required. 5.2.2 Weighting Sample Members The second factor is the weight given to each member in the sample. Four principal weighting schemes are used for security-market indexes: (1) a price-weighted index, (2) a market-valueweighted index, (3) an unweighted index, or what would be described as an equal-weighted index, and (4) a fundamental weighted index based on some operating variable like sales, earnings, or return on equity. We will discuss each of these in detail and consider examples of them. 5.2.3 Computational Procedure The final consideration is the computational procedure used. One alternative is to take a simple arithmetic mean of the various members in the index. Another is to compute an index and have all changes, whether in price or value, reported in terms of the basic index. Finally, some prefer using a geometric mean of the components rather than an arithmetic mean. 5.3 STOCK-MARKET INDEXES As mentioned previously, we hear a lot about what happens to the Dow Jones Industrial Average (DJIA) each day. You might also hear about other stock indexes, such as the S&P 500 index, the NASDAQ composite, or even the Nikkei Average of Japanese stocks. If you listen carefully, you will realize that these indexes experience different percentage changes (which is the way that the changes should be reported). Reasons for some differences are obvious, such as the DJIA versus the Nikkei Average, but others are not. In this section, we briefly review how the major series differ in terms of the characteristics discussed in the prior section, which will help you understand why the percent changes over time for alternative stock indexes should differ. We have organized the discussion of the indexes by the weighting of the sample of stocks. We begin with the price-weighted index because some of the most popular indexes are in this category. The next group is the value-weighted index, which is the technique currently used for most indexes. This is followed by the unweighted indexes, and finally the fundamental indexes.

CHAPTER SEVEN

Efficient Capital Markets

An efficient capital market is one in which security prices adjust rapidly to the arrival of new information, and, therefore, the current prices of securities reflect all information about the security. Some of the most interesting and important academic research during the past 30 years has analyzed whether our capital markets are efficient. This extensive research is important because its results have significant real-world implications for investors and portfolio managers. In addition, the question of whether capital markets are efficient is one of the most controversial areas in investment research. A new dimension has been added to the controversy because of the rapidly expanding research in behavioral finance that has major implications regarding the concept of efficient capital markets and has provided some intriguing insights on reasons for many of the anomalies identified. Because of its importance and controversy, you need to understand the meaning of the terms efficient capital markets and the efficient market hypothesis (EMH). You should understand the analysis performed to test the EMH and the results of studies that either support or contradict the hypothesis. Finally, you should be aware of the implications of these results when you analyze alternative investments and work to construct a portfolio. 149 WWW.YAZDANPRESS.COM We are considering the topic of efficient capital markets at this point for two reasons. First, the prior discussion indicated how the capital markets function, so now it seems natural to consider the efficiency of these markets in terms of how security prices react to new information. Second, the overall evidence on capital market efficiency is best described as mixed; some studies support the hypothesis, and others do not. The implications of these diverse results are important for you as an investor involved in analyzing securities, estimating intrinsic value, and building a portfolio. This chapter contains five major sections. The first discusses why we would expect capital markets to be efficient and the factors that contribute to an efficient market where the prices of securities reflect available information. The efficient market hypothesis has been divided into three subhypotheses to facilitate testing. The second section describes these three subhypotheses and the implications of each of them. The third section is the largest section because it contains a discussion of the results of numerous studies. This review of the research reveals that a large body of evidence supports the EMH, but a growing number of other studies do not support the hypotheses. In the fourth section, we discuss the concept of behavioral finance, the studies that have been done in this area related to efficient markets, and the conclusions as they relate to the EMH. The final section discusses what these results imply for an investor who uses either technical analysis or fundamental analysis or what they mean for a portfolio manager who has access to superior or inferior analysts. We conclude with a brief discussion of the evidence for markets in foreign countries. 6.1 WHY SHOULD CAPITAL MARKETS BE EFFICIENT? As noted earlier, in an efficient capital market, security prices adjust rapidly to the infusion of new information, and, therefore, current security prices fully reflect all available information. To be absolutely correct, this is referred to as an informationally efficient market. Although the idea of an efficient capital market is relatively straightforward, we often fail to consider why capital markets should be efficient. What set of assumptions imply an efficient capital market? An initial and important premise of an efficient market requires that a large number of profit-maximizing participants analyze and value securities, each independently of the others. A second assumption is that new information regarding securities comes to the market in a random fashion, and the timing of one announcement is generally independent of others.1 The third assumption is especially crucial: the buy and sell decisions of all those profit-maximizing investors cause security prices to adjust rapidly to reflect the effect of new information. Although the price adjustment may be imperfect, it is unbiased. This means that sometimes the market will over adjust and other times it will under adjust, but you cannot predict which will occur at any given time. Security prices adjust rapidly because the many profit-maximizing investors are competing against one another to profit from the new information.

The combined effect of (1) information coming in a random, independent, unpredictable fashion and (2) numerous competing investors adjusting stock prices rapidly to reflect this new information means that one would expect price changes to be independent and random. Clearly, the adjustment process requires a large number of investors following the movements of the security, analyzing the impact of new information on its value, and buying or selling the security until its price adjusts to reflect the new information. This scenario implies that informationally efficient markets require some minimum amount of trading and that more trading by numerous competing investors should cause a faster price adjustment, making the market more efficient. We will return to this need for trading and investor attention when we discuss some anomalies of the EMH. The reader is also reminded of the discussion in Chapter 4 regarding the significant increase in transactions and trading volume over the past decade as well as the reduction in the cost of trading. Finally, because security prices adjust to all new information, these security prices should reflect all information that is publicly available at any point in time. Therefore, the security prices that prevail at any time should be an unbiased reflection of all currently available information, including the risk involved in owning the security. Therefore, in an efficient market, the expected returns implicit in the current price of the security should reflect its risk, which means that investors who buy at these informationally efficient prices should receive a rate of return that is consistent with the perceived risk of the security. Put another way, in terms of the CAPM that is discussed in Chapter 8, all securities should lie on the SML such that their expected rates of return are consistent with their perceived risk. 6.2 ALTERNATIVE EFFICIENT MARKET HYPOTHESES Most of the early work related to efficient capital markets was based on the random walk hypothesis, which contended that changes in stock prices occurred randomly. This early academic work contained extensive empirical analysis without much theory behind it. An article by Fama (1970) attempted to formalize the theory and organize the growing empirical evidence. Fama presented the efficient market theory in terms of a fair game model, contending that investors can be confident that a current market price fully reflects all available information about a security and, therefore, the expected return based upon this price is consistent with its risk. In his original article, Fama divided the overall efficient market hypothesis (EMH) and the empirical tests of the hypothesis into three subhypotheses depending on the information set involved: (1) weak-form EMH, (2) semistrong-form EMH, and (3) strong-form EMH. In a subsequent review article, Fama (1991a) again divided the empirical results into three groups but shifted empirical results between the prior categories. Therefore, the following discussion uses the original categories, noted above, but organizes the presentation of results using the new categories. In the remainder of this section, we describe the three subhypotheses and the implications of each of them. As noted, the three subhypotheses are based on alternative information sets. In the following section, we briefly describe how researchers have tested these hypotheses and summarize the results of these tests. 6.2.1 Weak-Form Efficient Market Hypothesis The weak-form EMH assumes that current stock prices fully reflect all security market information, including the historical sequence of prices, rates of return, trading volume data, and other market-generated information, such as odd-lot transactions and transactions by marketmakers. Because it assumes that current market prices already reflect all past returns and any other security market information, this hypothesis implies that past rates of return and other Chapter 6: Efficient Capital Markets 151 WWW.YAZDANPRESS.COM historical market data should have no relationship with future rates of return (that is, rates of return should be independent). Therefore, this hypothesis contends that you should gain little from using any trading rule which indicates that you should buy or sell a security based on past rates of return or any other past security market data. 6.2.2 Semistrong-Form Efficient Market Hypothesis The semistrong-form EMH asserts that security prices adjust rapidly to the release of all public information; that is, current security prices fully reflect all public information. The semistrong hypothesis encompasses the weak-form hypothesis, because all the market information considered by the weak-form hypothesis, such as stock prices, rates of return, and trading volume, is public. Notably, public information also includes all nonmarket information, such as earnings and dividend announcements, price-to-earnings (P/E) ratios, dividend-yield (D/P) ratios, price-book value (P/BV) ratios, stock splits, news about the economy, and political news. This hypothesis implies that investors who base their decisions on any important new information after it is public should not derive above-average risk-adjusted profits from their transactions, considering the cost of trading because the security price should immediately reflect all such new public information. 6.2.3 Strong-Form Efficient Market Hypothesis The strong-form EMH contends that stock prices fully reflect all information from public and private sources. This means that no group of investors has monopolistic access to information relevant to the formation of prices. Therefore, this hypothesis contends that no group of investors should be able to consistently derive above-average risk-adjusted rates of return. The strong-form EMH encompasses both the weak-form and the semistrong-form EMH. Further, the strong-form EMH extends the assumption of efficient markets, in which prices adjust rapidly to the release of new public information, to assume perfect markets, in which all information is cost-free and available to everyone at the same time. 6.3 TESTS AND RESULTS OF EFFICIENT MARKET HYPOTHESES Now that you understand the three components of the EMH and what each of them implies regarding the effect on security prices of different sets of information, we can consider the tests used to see whether the data support the hypotheses. Therefore, in this section we discuss the specific tests and summarize the results of these tests. Like most hypotheses in finance and economics, the evidence on the EMH is mixed. Some studies have supported the hypotheses and indicate that capital markets are efficient. Results of other studies have revealed some anomalies related to these hypotheses, indicating results that do not support the hypotheses. 6.3.1 Weak-Form Hypothesis: Tests and Results Researchers have formulated two groups of tests of the weak-form EMH. The first category involves statistical tests of independence between rates of return. The second set of tests entails a comparison of risk–return results for trading rules that make investment decisions based on past market information relative to the results from a simple buy-and-hold policy, which assumes that you buy stock at the beginning of a test period and hold it to the end. Statistical Tests of Independence As discussed earlier, the EMH contends that security returns over time should be independent of one another because new information comes to the 152 Part 2: Developments in Investment Theory WWW.YAZDANPRESS.COM market in a random, independent fashion, and security prices adjust rapidly to this new information. Two major statistical tests have been employed to verify this independence. First, autocorrelation tests of independence measure the significance of positive or negative correlation in returns over time. Does the rate of return on day t correlate with the rate of return on day t − 1, t − 2, or t − 3?2 Those who believe that capital markets are efficient would expect insignificant correlations for all such combinations. Several researchers have examined the serial correlations among stock returns for several relatively short time horizons including 1 day, 4 days, 9 days, and 16 days. The results typically indicated insignificant correlation in stock returns over time. Some recent studies that considered portfolios of stocks of different market size have indicated that the autocorrelation is stronger for portfolios of small market size stocks. Therefore, although the older results tend to support the hypothesis, the more recent studies cast doubt on it for portfolios of small firms, although these results could be offset by the higher transaction costs of small-cap stocks and nonsynchronous trading for small-cap stocks. The second statistical test of independence as discussed by DeFusco et al. (2004), is the runs test. Given a series of price changes, each price change is either designated a plus (+) if it is an increase in price or a minus (–) if it is a decrease in price. The result is a set of pluses and minuses as follows: + + + – + – – + + – – + +. A run occurs when two consecutive changes are the same; two or more consecutive positive or negative price changes constitute one run. When the price changes in a different direction, such as when a negative price change is followed by a positive price change, the run ends and a new run may begin. To test for independence, you would compare the number of runs for a given series to the number in a table of expected values for the number of runs that should occur in a random series. Studies that have examined stock price runs have confirmed the independence of stock price changes over time. The actual number of runs for stock price series consistently fell into the range expected for a random series. Therefore, these statistical tests of stocks on the NYSE and on the NASDAQ market have likewise confirmed the independence of stock price changes over time. Although short-horizon stock returns (monthly, weekly, and daily) have generally supported the weak-form EMH, several studies that examined price changes for individual transactions on the NYSE found significant serial correlations. Some of the original studies indicated that the serial correlation meant that momentum could be used to generate excess risk-adjusted returns, but they also concluded that the substantial transaction costs wiped out the profits. In contrast, more recent studies that recognized the substantially lower transaction cost in the current environment as discussed in Chapter 4 indicate that return momentum can be a viable trading technique. Subsequently, Heston, Korajczyk, and Sadka (2010) found intraday patterns of returns and volume persisted for relatively long periods (40 trading days), and they attribute this to systematic trading and institutional fund flows. Tests of Trading Rules The second group of tests of the weak-form EMH were developed in response to the assertion that some of the prior statistical tests of independence were too rigid to identify the intricate price patterns examined by technical analysts. As we will discuss in Chapter 15, technical analysts do not expect a set number of positive or negative price changes as a signal of a move to a new equilibrium in the market. They typically look for a general consistency in the price trends over time. Such a trend might include both positive and negative changes. Therefore, technical analysts believed that their sophisticated trading rules could not be properly tested by rigid statistical tests. In response to this objection, investigators attempted to examine alternative technical trading rules through simulation. Advocates of an efficient market hypothesized that investors could not derive abnormal profits above a buy-and-hold policy using any trading rule that depended solely on past market information. The trading rule studies compared the risk–return results derived from trading-rule simulations, including transaction costs, to the results from a simple buy-and-hold policy. Three major pitfalls can negate the results of a trading-rule study: 1. The investigator should use only publicly available data when implementing the trading rule. As an example, the trading activities of some set of traders/investors for some period ending December 31 may not be publicly available until February 1. Therefore, you should not factor in information about the trading activity until the information is public. 2. When computing the returns from a trading rule, you should include all transaction costs involved in implementing the trading strategy because most trading rules involve many more transactions than a simple buy-and-hold policy. 3. You must adjust the results for risk because a trading rule might simply select a portfolio of high-risk securities that should experience higher returns. Researchers have encountered two operational problems in carrying out these tests of specific trading rules. First, some trading rules require too much subjective interpretation of data to simulate mechanically. Second, the almost infinite number of potential trading rules makes it impossible to test all of them. As a result, only the better-known technical trading rules that can be programmed into a computer have been examined. Another factor that should be recognized is that the simulation studies have typically been restricted to relatively simple trading rules, which many technicians contend are rather naïve. In addition, many of the early studies employed readily available data from the NYSE, which is biased toward well-known, heavily traded stocks that certainly should trade in efficient markets. Recall that markets should be more efficient when there are numerous aggressive, profitmaximizing investors attempting to adjust stock prices to reflect new information, so market efficiency will be related to trading volume. Specifically, more trading in a security should promote market efficiency.

Alternatively, for securities with relatively few stockholders and limited trading activity, the market could be inefficient simply because fewer investors would be analyzing the effect of any new information. This limited interest would result in insufficient trading activity to move the price of the security quickly to a new equilibrium value that reflects the new information. Therefore, using only active, heavily traded stocks when testing a trading rule could bias the results toward finding efficiency. Results of Simulations of Specific Trading Rules One of the most popular trading techniques is the filter rule, wherein an investor trades a stock when the price change exceeds a filter value set for it. As an example, an investor using a 5 percent filter would identify a positive breakout if the stock were to rise 5 percent from some base, suggesting that the stock price would continue to rise. A technician would acquire the stock to take advantage of the expected increase. In contrast, a 5 percent decline from some peak price would be considered a negative breakout, and the technician would expect a further price decline and would sell any holdings of the stock and possibly even sell the stock short. Studies of this trading rule have used a range of filters from 0.5 percent to 50 percent. The results indicated that small filters would yield above-average profits before taking account of trading commissions. However, small filters generate numerous trades and, therefore, substantial trading costs. When the pre-2000 trading costs were considered, all the trading profits turned to losses. It is possible that using recent lower trading costs (post-2011), the results could be different. Alternatively, trading using larger filters did not yield returns above those of a simple buy-and-hold policy. 154 Part 2: Developments in Investment Theory WWW.YAZDANPRESS.COM Researchers have simulated other trading rules that used past market data other than stock prices. Trading rules have been devised that consider advanced-decline ratios, short sales, short positions, and specialist activities.3 These simulation tests have generated mixed results. Most of the early studies using higher commission fees suggested that these trading rules generally would not outperform a buy-and-hold policy on a risk-adjusted basis after commissions. In contrast, several recent studies have indicated support for specific trading rules. Therefore, most evidence from simulations of specific trading rules indicates that most trading rules tested have not been able to beat a buy-and-hold policy. Therefore, the early test results generally support the weak-form EMH, but the results are clearly not unanimous, especially if one considers the substantially lower commissions that currently exist. 6.3.2

Semistrong-Form Hypothesis: Tests and Results Recall that the semistrong-form EMH asserts that security prices adjust rapidly to the release of all public information; that is, security prices fully reflect all public information. Studies that have tested the semistrong-form EMH can be divided into the following sets of studies: 1. Studies to predict future rates of return using available public information beyond pure market information such as prices and trading volume considered in the weak-form tests. These studies can involve either time-series analysis of returns or the cross-section distribution of returns for individual stocks. Advocates of the EMH contend that it would not be possible to predict future returns using past returns or to predict the distribution of future returns (e.g., the top quartile or decile of returns) using public information. 2. Event studies that examine how fast stock prices adjust to specific significant economic events. A corollary approach would be to test whether it is possible to invest in a security after the public announcement of a significant event (e.g., earnings, stock splits, major economic data) and experience significant abnormal rates of return. Again, advocates of the EMH would expect security prices to adjust rapidly, such that it would not be possible for investors to experience superior risk-adjusted returns by investing after the public announcement and paying normal transaction costs. Adjustment for Market Effects For any of these tests, you need to adjust the security's rates of return for the rates of return of the overall market during the period considered. The point is that a 5 percent return in a stock during the period surrounding an announcement is meaningless until you know what the aggregate stock market did during the same period and how this stock normally acts under such conditions. If the market had experienced a 10 percent return during this announcement period, the 5 percent return for the stock may be lower than expected. Early studies (pre-1980) generally recognized the need to make adjustments for market movements by assuming that the individual stocks should experience returns equal to the aggregate stock market. Thus, the market-adjustment process simply entailed subtracting the market return from the return for the individual security to derive its abnormal rate of return, as follows: 6.1 ARit = Rit − Rmt where: ARit = abnormal rate of return on security i during period t Rit = rate of return on security i during period t Rmt = rate of return on a market index during period t In the example where the stock experienced a 5 percent increase while the market increased 10 percent, the stock's abnormal return would be minus 5 percent. 3 Many of these trading rules are discussed in Chapter

15, which deals with technical analysis. Chapter 6: Efficient Capital Markets 155 WWW.YAZDANPRESS.COM Recent authors have adjusted the rates of return for securities by an amount different from the market rate of return because they recognize that, based on work with the CAPM, all stocks do not change by the same amount as the market. That is, as will be discussed in Chapter 8, some stocks are more volatile than the market, and some are less volatile. These possibilities mean that you must determine an expected rate of return for the stock based on the market rate of return and the stock's relationship with the market (its beta). As an example, suppose a stock is generally 20 percent more volatile than the market (that is, it has a beta of 1.20). In such a case, if the market experiences a 10 percent rate of return, you would expect this stock to experience a 12 percent rate of return. Therefore, you would determine the abnormal rate of return by computing the difference between the stock's actual rate of return and its expected rate of return as follows: 6.2 ARit = Rit − E(Rit) where: EðRitÞ = the expected rate of return for stock i during period t based on the market rate of return and the stock's normal relationship with the market ðits betaÞ Continuing with the example, if the stock that was expected to have a 12 percent return (based on a market return of 10 percent and a stock beta of 1.20) had only a 5 percent return, its abnormal rate of return during the period would be minus 7 percent. Over the normal long-run period, you would expect the abnormal returns for a stock to sum to zero. Specifically, during one period the returns may exceed expectations and the next period they may fall short of expectations. Alternate Semistrong Tests Given this understanding of the market adjustment, recall that there are two sets of tests of the semistrong-form EMH. The first set are referred to as return prediction studies. In these studies, investigators attempt to predict the time series of future rates of return for individual stocks or the aggregate market using public information. For example, is it possible to predict abnormal returns over time for the market based on public information such as changes in the aggregate dividend yield or the risk premium spread for bonds? Another example would be event studies that examine abnormal rates of return for a period immediately after an announcement of a significant economic event, such as a stock split, a proposed merger, or a stock or bond issue, to determine whether an investor can derive above-average risk-adjusted rates of return by investing after the release of public information. Another set of studies attempt to predict cross-sectional returns by examining public information regarding individual stocks that will allow investors to predict the cross-sectional distribution of future risk-adjusted rates of return. For example, they test whether it is possible to use variables such as the price-earnings ratio, market value size, the price/book-value ratio, the P/E/growth rate (PEG) ratio, or the dividend yield to predict which stocks will experience above-average (e.g., top quartile) or below-average risk-adjusted rates of return in the future. In both sets of tests, the emphasis is on the analysis of abnormal rates of return that deviate from long-term expectations. Results of Return Prediction Studies The time-series analysis assumes that in an efficient market the best estimate of future rates of return will be the long-run historical rates of return. The tests attempt to determine whether any public information will provide superior estimates of returns for a short-run horizon (one to six months) or a long-run horizon (one to five years). Risk Premium Proxies These studies have indicated limited success in predicting shorthorizon returns, but the analysis of long-horizon returns has been quite successful. A prime example is dividend yield studies. After postulating that the aggregate dividend yield (D/P) 156 Part 2: Developments in Investment Theory WWW.YAZDANPRESS.COM was a proxy for the risk premium on stocks, they found a positive relationship between the D/P and future long-run stock market returns. In addition, several studies have considered two variables related to the term structure of interest rates: (1) a default spread, which is the difference between the yields on lower-grade and Aaa-rated long-term corporate bonds (this spread has been used in earlier chapters of this book as a proxy for a market risk premium), and (2) the term structure spread, which is the difference between the long-term Treasury bond yield and the yield on one-month Treasury bills. These variables have been used to predict stock returns and bond returns. Similar variables have also been useful for predicting returns for foreign common stocks. The reasoning for these empirical results is as follows: When the two most significant variables—the dividend yield (D/P) and the bond default spread—are high, it implies that investors are requiring a high return on stocks and bonds. Notably, this occurs during poor economic environments that imply a low-wealth environment wherein investors perceive an increase in risk for investments. As a result, for investors to invest and shift consumption from the present to the future, they will require a high rate of return (i.e., a high-risk premium) that will cause a decline in prices for risky assets. Therefore, if you invest during this risk-averse period, your subsequent returns will be above normal. In contrast, when dividend yields and yield spreads are small, it implies that investors have reduced their risk premium and required rates of return, and, therefore, their future returns will be below normal. The results of studies that support this expectation would be evidence against the EMH because they indicate you can use public information on dividend yields and yield spreads to predict future abnormal returns. Quarterly Earnings Reports Studies that address quarterly reports are considered part of the times-series analysis. Specifically, these studies examine whether it is possible to predict future individual stock returns based on publicly available information on changes in quarterly earnings that differed from expectations. The results generally indicated that there were abnormal stock returns during the 13 or 26 weeks following the announcement of a large unanticipated earnings change—referred to as an earnings surprise. These results indicate that an earnings surprise is not instantaneously reflected in security prices. An extensive analysis by Rendleman, Jones, and Latané (1982) and a follow-up by Jones, Rendleman, and Latané (1985) using a large sample and daily data from 20 days before a quarterly earnings announcement to 90 days after the announcement indicated that 31 percent of the total response in stock returns came before the earnings announcement, 18 percent on the day of the announcement, and 51 percent after the announcement. Several subsequent studies by Benesh and Peterson (1986), Bernard and Thomas (1989), and Baruch (1989) contended that the reason for the stock price drift was the earnings revisions that followed the earnings surprises and these revisions contributed to the positive correlations of prices. In summary, these results indicate that the market has not adjusted stock prices to reflect the release of quarterly earnings surprises as fast as expected by the semistrong EMH, which implies that earnings surprises and earnings revisions can be used to predict returns for individual stocks. These results are evidence against the EMH.4 These results have also been enhanced by research from Campbell, Ramadorai, and Schwartz (2009), that showed institutions are able to anticipate earning surprises and also a study by Vega (2006) which contents that the post-announcement drift is also affected by whether the information is associated with the arrival rate of informed and uniformed traders. It was also determined that earning surprises have a larger affect on small firms.

In addition, there have been some "calendar studies" that questioned whether some regularities in the rates of return during the calendar year would allow investors to predict returns on stocks. This research included numerous studies on "the January anomaly" and studies that consider a variety of other daily and weekly regularities. The January Anomaly Several years ago, Branch (1977) and Branch and Chang (1985) proposed a unique trading rule for those interested in taking advantage of tax selling. Investors (including institutions) tend to engage in tax selling toward the end of the year to establish losses on stocks that have declined. After the new year, the tendency is to reacquire these stocks or to buy similar stocks that look attractive. This scenario would produce downward pressure on stock prices in late November and December and positive pressure in early January. Such a seasonal pattern is inconsistent with the EMH since it should be eliminated by arbitrageurs who would buy in December and sell in early January. A supporter of the hypothesis found that December trading volume was abnormally high for stocks that had declined during the previous year and that significant abnormal returns occurred during January for stocks that had experienced losses during the prior year. It was concluded that, because of transaction costs, arbitrageurs must not be eliminating the January taxselling anomaly. Subsequent analysis showed that most of the January effect was concentrated in the first week of trading, particularly on the first day of the year. Several studies provided support for a January effect but were inconsistent with the tax-selling hypothesis because of what happened in foreign countries that did not have our tax laws or a December year-end. They found abnormal returns in January, but the results could not be explained by tax laws. It has also been shown that the classic relationship between risk and return is strongest during January and there is a year-end trading volume bulge in late December–early January. Another facet of the January effect (refered to as "the other January effect") is related to aggregate market returns where in it is contended that stock market returns in January are a predicter to the return over the next 11 months of the year. A study by Cooper, McConnell, and Outchinnikou (2006) finds strong support for this contention. Other Calendar Effects Several other "calendar" effects have been examined, including a monthly effect, a weekend/day-of-the-week effect, and an intraday effect. One study found a significant monthly effect wherein all the market's cumulative advance occurred during the first half of trading months. An analysis of the weekend effect found that the mean return for Monday was significantly negative during five-year subperiods and a total period. In contrast, the average return for the other four days was positive. A study decomposed the Monday effect that is typically measured from

Friday close to Monday close into a weekend effect (from Friday close to Monday open), and a pure Monday trading effect (from Monday open to the Monday close). It was shown that the negative Monday effect found in prior studies actually occurs from the Friday close to the Monday open (it is really a weekend effect). After adjusting for the weekend effect, the pure Monday trading effect was positive. Subsequently, it was shown that the Monday effect was on average positive in January and negative for all other months. Finally, for large firms, the negative Monday effect occurred before the market opened (it was a weekend effect), whereas for smaller firms most of the negative Monday effect occurred during the day on Monday (it was a Monday trading effect). Predicting Cross-Sectional Returns Assuming an efficient market, all securities should have equal risk-adjusted returns because security prices should reflect all public information that would influence the security's risk. Therefore, studies in this category attempt to determine if 158 Part 2: Developments in Investment Theory WWW.YAZDANPRESS.COM you can use public information to predict what stocks will enjoy above-average or belowaverage risk-adjusted returns. These studies typically examine the usefulness of alternative measures of size or quality to rank stocks in terms of risk-adjusted returns. Keep in mind that all of these tests involve a joint hypothesis because they not only consider the efficiency of the market but also are dependent on the asset pricing model that provides the measure of risk used in the test. Specifically, if a test determines that it is possible to predict risk-adjusted returns, these results could occur because the market is not efficient, or they could be because the measure of risk is faulty and, therefore, the measures of risk-adjusted returns are wrong. Price-Earnings Ratios Several studies beginning with Basu (1977) have examined the relationship between the historical price-earnings (P/E) ratios for stocks and the returns on the stocks. Some have suggested that low P/E stocks will outperform high P/E stocks because growth companies enjoy high P/E ratios, but the market tends to overestimate the growth potential and thus overvalues these growth companies, while undervaluing low-growth firms with low P/E ratios. A relationship between the historical P/E ratios and subsequent risk-adjusted market performance would constitute evidence against the semistrong EMH, because it would imply that investors could use publicly available information regarding P/E ratios to predict future abnormal returns. Performance measures that consider both return and risk indicated that low P/E ratio stocks experienced superior risk-adjusted results relative to the market, whereas high P/E ratio stocks had significantly inferior risk-adjusted results.5 Subsequent analysis concluded that publicly available P/E ratios possess valuable information regarding future returns, which is inconsistent with semistrong efficiency. Peavy and Goodman (1983) examined P/E ratios with adjustments for firm size, industry effects, and infrequent trading and likewise found that the risk-adjusted returns for stocks in the lowest P/E ratio quintile were superior to those in the highest P/E ratio quintile. Price-Earnings/Growth Rate (PEG) Ratios During the past decade, there has been a significant increase in the use of the ratio of a stock's price-earnings ratio divided by the firm's expected growth rate of earnings (referred to as the PEG ratio) as a relative valuation tool, especially for stocks of growth companies that have P/E ratios substantially above average. Advocates of the PEG ratio hypothesize an inverse relationship between the PEG ratio and subsequent rates of return—that is, they expect that stocks with relatively low PEG ratios (i.e., less than one) will experience above-average rates of return while stocks with relatively high PEG ratios (i.e., in excess of three or four) will have below-average rates of return. A study by Peters (1991) using quarterly rebalancing supported the hypothesis of an inverse relationship. These results would constitute an anomaly and would not support the EMH. A subsequent study by Reilly and Marshall (1999) assumed annual rebalancing and divided the sample on the basis of a risk measure (beta), market value size, and by expected growth rate. Except for stocks with low betas and very low expected growth rates, the results were not consistent with the hypothesis of an inverse relationship between the PEG ratio and subsequent rates of return. In summary, the results related to using the PEG ratio to select stocks are mixed—several studies that assume either monthly or quarterly rebalancing indicate an anomaly because the authors use public information and derive above-average rates of return. In contrast, a study with more realistic annual rebalancing indicated that no consistent relationship exists between the PEG ratio and subsequent rates of return. The Size Effect Banz (1981) examined the impact of size (measured by total market value) on the risk-adjusted rates of return. The risk-adjusted returns for extended periods (20 to 35 years) indicated that the small firms consistently experienced significantly larger risk-adjusted returns than the larger firms. Reinganum (1981) contended that it was the size, not the P/E ratio, that caused the results discussed in the prior subsection, but this contention was disputed by Basu (1983). Recall that abnormal returns may occur because the markets are inefficient or because the market model provides incorrect estimates of risk and expected returns. It was suggested that the riskiness of the small firms was improperly measured because small firms are traded less frequently. An alternative risk measure technique confirmed that the small firms had much higher risk than previously measured, but the consideration of the higher betas still did not account for the large difference in rates of return. A study by Stoll and Whaley (1983) that examined the impact of transaction costs confirmed the size effect but also found that firms with small market value generally have low stock prices. Because transaction costs vary inversely with price per share, these costs must be considered when examining the small-firm effect. They found a significant difference in the percentage total transaction cost for large firms (2.71 percent) versus small firms (6.77 percent). This differential in transaction costs, assuming frequent trading, can have a significant impact on the results. Assuming daily transactions, the original small-firm effects are reversed. The point is, size-effect studies must consider realistic transaction costs and specify holding period assumptions. A study by Reinganum (1983) that considered both factors over long periods demonstrated that infrequent rebalancing (about once a year) is almost ideal—the results beat long-run buy-and-hold and avoid frequent rebalancing that causes excess costs. In summary, small firms outperformed large firms after considering higher risk and realistic transaction costs (assuming annual rebalancing). Most studies on the size effect employed large databases and long time periods (over 50 years) to show that this phenomenon has existed for many years. In contrast, a study that examined the performance over various intervals of time concluded that the small-firm effect is not stable. During most periods investigators found the negative relationship between size and return; but, during selected periods (such as 1967 to 1975), they found that large firms outperformed the small firms. Notably, this positive relationship held during the following recent periods: 1984–1987; 1989–1990; 1995–1998; and during 2005–2009 on a risk-adjusted basis.6 Reinganum (1992) acknowledges this instability but contends that the small-firm effect is still a long-run phenomenon. In summary, firm size is a major efficient market anomaly. The two strongest explanations are higher risk measurements due to infrequent trading and the higher transaction costs. Depending on the frequency of trading, these two factors may account for much of the differential. Keim (1983) also related it to seasonality. These results indicate that the size effect must be considered in any event study that considers long time periods and contains a sample of firms with significantly different market values. Neglected Firms and Trading Activity Arbel and Strebel (1983) considered an additional influence beyond size—attention or neglect. They measured attention in terms of the number of analysts who regularly follow a stock and divided the stocks into three groups: (1) highly followed, (2) moderately followed, and (3) neglected. They confirmed the small-firm effect but also found a neglected-firm effect caused by the lack of information and limited institutional interest. The neglected-firm concept applied across size classes. Contrary results are reported by Beard and Sias (1997) who found no evidence of a neglected firm premium after controlling for capitalization. James and Edmister (1983) examined the impact of trading volume by considering the relationship between returns, market value, and trading activity. The results confirmed the relationship between size and rates of return, but the results indicated no significant difference between the mean returns of the highest and lowest trading activity portfolios. A subsequent study hypothesized that firms with less information require higher returns. Using the period of listing as a proxy for information, they found a negative relationship between returns and the period of listing after adjusting for firm size and the January effect. Book Value—Market Value Ratio This ratio relates the book value (BV) of a firm's equity to the market value (MV) of its equity. Rosenberg, Reid, and Lanstein (1985) found a significant positive relationship between current values for this ratio and future stock returns and contended that such a relationship between available public information on the BV/MV ratio and future returns was evidence against the EMH.7 Strong support for this ratio was provided by Fama and French (1992) who evaluated the joint effects of market beta, size, E/P ratio, leverage, and the BV/MV ratio (referred to as BE/ME) on a cross section of average returns. They analyzed the hypothesized positive relationship between beta and expected returns and found that this positive relationship held pre-1969 but disappeared during the period 1963 to 1990. In contrast, the negative relationship between size and average return was significant by itself and significant after inclusion of other variables. In addition, they found a significant positive relationship between the BV/MV ratio and average return that persisted even when other variables are included. Most importantly, both size and the BV/MV ratio are significant when included together and they dominate other ratios. Specifically, although leverage and the E/P ratio were significant by themselves or with size, they become insignificant when both size and the BV/MV ratio are considered. The results in Exhibit 6.1 show the separate and combined effect of the two variables. As shown, going across the Small-ME (small size) row, BV/MV captures strong variation in average returns (0.70 to 1.92 percent). Alternatively, controlling for the BV/MV ratio leaves a size effect in average returns (the high BV/MV results decline from 1.92 to 1.18 percent when going from small to large). These positive results for the BV/MV ratio were replicated for returns on Japanese stocks. In summary, studies that have used publicly available ratios to predict the cross section of expected returns for stocks have provided substantial evidence in conflict with the semistrongform EMH. Significant results were found for P/E ratios, market value size, and BV/MV ratios. Although the research by Fama and French indicated that the optimal combination appears to be size and the BV/MV ratio, a study by Jensen, Johnson, and Mercer (1997) indicates that this combination only works during periods of expansive monetary policy. Results of Event Studies Recall that the intent of event studies is to examine abnormal rates of return surrounding significant economic information. Those who advocate the EMH would expect returns to adjust quickly to announcements of new information such that investors cannot experience positive abnormal rates of return by acting after the announcement. Because of space constraints, we can only summarize the results for some of the more popular events considered. The discussion of results is organized by event or item of public information. Specifically, we will examine the price movements and profit potential surrounding stock splits, the sale of initial public offerings, exchange listings, unexpected world or economic events, and the announcements of significant accounting changes. Notably, the results for most of these studies have supported the semistrong-form EMH.

Stock Split Studies Many investors believe that the prices of stocks that split will increase in value because the shares are priced lower, which increases demand for them. In contrast, advocates of efficient markets would not expect a change in value because the firm has simply issued additional stock and nothing fundamentally affecting the value of the firm has occurred. The classic study by Fama, Fisher, Jensen, and Roll (1969), referred to hereafter as FFJR, hypothesized no significant price change following a stock split, because any relevant information (such as earnings growth) that caused the split would have already been discounted. The FFJR study analyzed abnormal price movements surrounding the time of the split and divided the stock split sample into those stocks that did or did not raise their dividends. Both groups experienced positive abnormal price changes prior to the split. Stocks that split but did not increase their dividend experienced abnormal price declines following the split and within 12 months lost all their accumulated abnormal gains. In contrast, stocks that split and increased their dividend experienced no abnormal returns after the split. These results support the semistrong EMH because they indicate that investors cannot gain from the information on a stock split after the public announcement. These results were confirmed by most (but not all) subsequent studies. In summary, most studies found no short-run or long-run positive impact on security returns because of a stock split, although the results are not unanimous. Exhibit 6.1 Average Monthly Returns on Portfolios Formed on Size and Book-to-Market Equity; Stocks Sorted by ME (Down) and Then BE/ME (Across); July 1963 to December 1990 In June of each year t, the NYSE, AMEX, and NASDAQ stocks that meet the CRSP-COMPUSTAT data requirements are allocated to 10 size portfolios using the NYSE size (ME) breakpoints. The NYSE, AMEX, and NASDAQ stocks in each size decile are then sorted into 10 BE/ME portfolios using the book-to-market ratios for year t – 1. BE/ME is the book value of common equity plus balance-sheet deferred taxes for fiscal year t – 1, over market equity for December of year t – 1. The equal-weighted monthly portfolio returns are then calculated for July of year t to June of year t + 1. Average monthly return is the time-series average of the monthly equal-weighted portfolio returns (in percent). The All column shows average returns for equal-weighted size decile portfolios. The All row shows average returns for equal-weighted portfolios of the stocks in each BE/ME group. BOOK-TO-MARKET PORTFOLIOS All Low 2 3 4 5 6 7 8 9 High All 1.23 0.64 0.98 1.06 1.17 1.24 1.26 1.39 1.40 1.50 1.63 Small-ME 1.47 0.70 1.14 1.20 1.43 1.56 1.51 1.70 1.71 1.82 1.92 ME-2 1.22 0.43 1.05 0.96 1.19 1.33 1.19 1.58 1.28 1.43 1.79 ME-3 1.22 0.56 0.88 1.23 0.95 1.36 1.30 1.30 1.40 1.54 1.60 ME-4 1.19 0.39 0.72 1.06 1.36 1.13 1.21 1.34 1.59 1.51 1.47 ME-5 1.24 0.88 0.65 1.08 1.47 1.13 1.43 1.44 1.26 1.52 1.49 ME-6 1.15 0.70 0.98 1.14 1.23 0.94 1.27 1.19 1.19 1.24 1.50 ME-7 1.07 0.95 1.00 0.99 0.83 0.99 1.13 0.99 1.16 1.10 1.47 ME-8 1.08 0.66 1.13 0.91 0.95 0.99 1.01 1.15 1.05 1.29 1.55 ME-9 0.95 0.44 0.89 0.92 1.00 1.05 0.93 0.82 1.11 1.04 1.22 Large-ME 0.89 0.93 0.88 0.84 0.71 0.79 0.83 0.81 0.96 0.97 1.18 Source: Eugene F. Fama and Kenneth French, “The Cross Section of Expected Stock Returns” Journal of Finance 47, no. 2 (June

1992): 446. Reprinted with permission of Blackwell Publishing. 162 Part 2: Developments in Investment Theory WWW.YAZDANPRESS.COM Initial Public Offerings (IPOs) During the past 20 years, a number of closely held companies have gone public by selling some of their common stock. Because of uncertainty about the appropriate offering price and the risk involved in underwriting such issues, it has been hypothesized that the underwriters would tend to underprice these new issues. Given this general expectation of underpricing, the studies in this area have generally considered three sets of questions: (1) How great is the underpricing on average? Does the underpricing vary over time? If so, why? (2) What factors cause different amounts of underpricing for alternative issues? (3) How fast does the market adjust the price for the underpricing? The answer to the first question is an average underpricing of about 17 percent, but it varies over time as shown by the results in Exhibit 6.2 for the total period 1980–2010 and for various subperiods. The major variables that cause differential underpricing seem to be various risk measures, the size of the firm, the prestige of the underwriter, and the status of the firm's accounting firm. On the question of direct interest to the EMH, results in Miller and Reilly (1987) and Ibbotson, Sindelar, and Ritter (1994) indicate that the price adjustment to the underpricing takes place within one day after the offering. Therefore, it appears that some underpricing occurs based on the original offering price, but the ones who benefit from this underpricing are basically the investors who receive allocations of the original issue. More specifically, institutional investors captured most (70 percent) of the short-term profits. This rapid adjustment of the initial underpricing would support the semistrong EMH. Finally, studies by Ritter (1991); Carter, Dark, and Singh (1998); and Loughran and Ritter (1995) that examined the long-run returns on IPOs indicate that investors who acquire the stock after the initial adjustment do not experience positive long-run abnormal returns. Exchange Listing A significant economic event for a firm is listing its stock on a national exchange, especially the NYSE. Such a listing is expected to increase the market liquidity of the stock and add to its prestige. An important question is, can an investor derive abnormal returns from investing in the stock when a new listing is announced or around the time of the actual listing? The results regarding abnormal returns from such investing were mixed. All the studies agreed that (1) the stocks' prices increased before any listing announcements, and (2) stock prices consistently declined after the actual listing. The crucial question is: What happens between the announcement of the application for listing and the actual listing (a period of four to six weeks)? A study by McConnell and Sanger (1989) points toward profit opportunities immediately after the announcement that a firm is applying for listing and there is the possibility of excess returns from price declines after the actual listing. Finally, studies that have examined the impact of listing on the risk of the securities found no significant change in systematic risk or the firm's cost of equity. In summary, because listing studies provide evidence of short-run profit opportunities for investors using public information, these studies would not support the semistrong-form EMH. Unexpected World Events and Economic News The results of several studies that examined the response of security prices to world or economic news have supported the semistrongform EMH. An analysis of the reaction of stock prices to unexpected world events, such as the Eisenhower heart attack, the Kennedy assassination, and military events, found that prices adjusted to the news before the market opened or before it reopened after the announcement (generally, as with the World Trade Center attack, the Exchanges are closed immediately for various time periods—e.g., one to four days). A study by Pierce and Roley (1985) that examined the response of stock prices to announcements about money supply, inflation, real economic activity, and the discount rate found an impact that did not persist beyond the announcement day. Finally, Jain (1988) did an analysis of an hourly response of stock returns and trading volume to surprise announcements and found that unexpected information about money supply impacted stock prices within one hour. For a review of studies that considered the impact of news on individual stocks, see Chan (2003). Announcements of Accounting Changes Numerous studies have analyzed the impact of announcements of accounting changes on stock prices. In efficient markets, security prices Exhibit 6.2 Number of Offerings, Average First-Day Returns, and Gross Proceeds of Initial Public Offerings in 1980–2010 Year Number of Offerings1 Average First-day Return2 Gross Proceeds, $ Millions3 1980 75 13.9% 934 1981 197 6.2% 2,367 1982 82 10.6% 1,064 1983 524 8.9% 11,332 1984 222 2.5% 2,841 1985 214 6.2% 5,125 1986 481 6.0% 15,793 1987 344 5.6% 13,300 1988 130 5.4% 4,141 1989 122 7.8% 5,406 1990 115 10.5% 4,325 1991 295 11.7% 16,602 1992 416 10.2% 22,678 1993 527 12.7% 31,599 1994 412 9.8% 17,560 1995 461 21.1% 30,230 1996 688 17.2% 42,425 1997 487 14.0% 32,441 1998 318 20.2% 34,614 1999 486 69.7% 64,927 2000 382 56.2% 65,088 2001 79 14.2% 34,241 2002 70 8.6% 22,136

2003 67 12.3% 10,068 2004 184 12.2% 32,269 2005 168 10.1% 28,593 2006 162 11.9% 30,648 2007 162 13.8% 35,762 2008 21 6.4% 22,762 2009 43 10.6% 13,307 2010 100 8.8% 31,291 1980–89 2,391 6.8% 62,303 1990–99 4,205 21.0% 297,441 2000–10 1,438 23.4% 326,165 1980–2010 8,034 17.1% 685,909 1 Beginning in 1980, the number of offerings excludes IPOs with an offer price of less than $5.00, ADRs, best efforts, units, and Regulation A offers (small issues, raising less than $1.5 million during the 1980s), real estate investment trusts (REITs), partnerships, and closed-end funds. Banks and S&Ls and non-CRSP-listed IPOs are included. 2 First-day returns are computed as the percentage return from the offering price to the first closing market price. 3 Gross proceeds exclude overallotment options but include the international tranche, if any. Source: Jay R. Ritter, "Summary Statistics on 1980–2010 Initial Public Offerings with an Offer Price of $5.00 or More." (University of Florida, January 2011). 164 Part 2: Developments in Investment Theory WWW.YAZDANPRESS.COM should react quickly and predictably to announcements of accounting changes that affect the economic value of the firm. An accounting change that affects reported earnings but has no economic significance should not affect stock prices. For example, when a firm changes its depreciation accounting method for reporting purposes from accelerated to straight line, the firm should experience an increase in reported earnings, but there is no economic consequence. An analysis of stock price movements surrounding this specific accounting change supported the EMH because there were no positive price changes following the change. In fact, there were some negative price changes because firms making such an accounting change are typically performing poorly. During periods of high inflation, many firms will change their inventory method from firstin, first-out (FIFO) to last-in, first-out (LIFO), which causes a decline in reported earnings but benefits the firm because it reduces the firm's taxable earnings and, therefore, tax expenses. Advocates of efficient markets would expect positive price changes because of the tax savings, and study results confirmed this expectation. Therefore, studies such as those by Bernard and Thomas (1990) and Ou and Penman (1989) indicate that the securities markets react quite rapidly to accounting changes and adjust security prices as expected on the basis of changes in true value (that is, analysts pierce the accounting veil and value securities on the basis of relevant economic events). Corporate Events Corporate finance events such as mergers and acquisitions, spin-offs, reorganization, and various security offerings (common stock, straight bonds, convertible bonds) have been examined, relative to two general questions: (1) What is the market impact of these alternative events? (2) How fast does the market adjust the security prices? Regarding the reaction to corporate events, the answer is very consistent—stock prices react as one would expect based on the underlying economic impact of the action. For example, the reaction to mergers is that the stock of the firm being acquired increases in line with the premium offered by the acquiring firm, whereas the stock of the acquiring firm typically declines because of the concern that they overpaid for the firm. On the question of speed of reaction, the evidence indicates fairly rapid adjustment—that is, the adjustment period declines as shorter interval data are analyzed (using daily data, most studies find that the price adjustment is completed in about three days). Studies related to financing decisions are reviewed by Smith (1986). Studies on corporate control that consider mergers and reorganizations are reviewed by Jensen and Warner (1988). Numerous corporate spin-offs have generated interesting stock performance as shown by Desai and Jain (1999) and Chemmanur and Yan (2004). Summary on the Semistrong-Form EMH Clearly, the evidence from tests of the semistrong EMH is mixed. The hypothesis receives almost unanimous support from the numerous event studies on a range of events including stock splits, initial public offerings, world events and economic news, accounting changes, and a variety of corporate finance events. About the only mixed results come from exchange listing studies. In sharp contrast, the numerous studies on predicting rates of return over time or for a cross section of stocks presented evidence counter to semistrong efficiency. This included time-series studies on risk premiums, calendar patterns, and quarterly earnings surprises. Similarly, the results for cross-sectional predictors such as size, the BV/MV ratio (when there is expansive monetary policy), and P/E ratios indicated anomalies that are not consistent with market efficiency. 6.3.3 Strong-Form Hypothesis: Tests and Results The strong-form EMH contends that stock prices fully reflect all information, public and private. This implies that no group of investors has access to private information that will allow them to consistently experience above-average profits. This extremely rigid hypothesis requires Chapter 6: Efficient Capital Markets 165 WWW.YAZDANPRESS.COM not only that stock prices must adjust rapidly to new public information but also that no group has access to private information. Tests of the strong-form EMH have analyzed returns over time for different identifiable investment groups to determine whether any group consistently received above-average risk-adjusted returns. Such a group must have access to and act upon important private information or an ability to act on public information before other investors, which would indicate that security prices were not adjusting rapidly to all new information. Investigators have tested this form of the EMH by analyzing the performance of the following three major groups of investors: (1) corporate insiders, (2) security analysts at Value Line and elsewhere, and (3) professional money managers. Prior editions of this book included tests that considered stock exchange specialists. This discussion is not included in this edition because the discussion in Chapter 4 indicates that the specialist involvement in stock trading is currently almost nonexistent due to the significant growth of electronic trading. Corporate Insider Trading Corporate insiders are required to report monthly to the SEC on their transactions (purchases or sales) in the stock of the firm for which they are insiders. Insiders include major corporate officers, members of the board of directors, and owners of 10 percent or more of any equity class of securities. About six weeks after the reporting period, this insider trading information is made public by the SEC. These insider trading data have been used to identify how corporate insiders have traded and determine whether they bought on balance before abnormally good price movements and sold on balance before poor market periods for their stock. The results of studies including Chowdhury, Howe, and Lin (1993) and Pettit and Venkatesh (1995) have generally indicated that corporate insiders consistently enjoyed above-average profits, heavily dependent on selling prior to low returns and not selling before strong returns. This implies that many insiders had private information from which they derived above-average returns on their company stock. In addition, an earlier study found that public investors who consistently traded with the insiders based on announced insider transactions would have enjoyed excess risk-adjusted returns (after commissions), although a subsequent study concluded that the market had eliminated this inefficiency after considering total transaction costs. Unfortunately, there are no recent studies that have examined this question assuming the very low transaction costs since 2006. Overall, these results provide mixed support for the EMH because several studies indicate that insiders experience abnormal profits, while subsequent studies pre-2006 indicate it is no longer possible for noninsiders to use this information to generate excess returns. Notably, because of investor interest in these insider trading data as a result of academic research, The Wall Street Journal currently publishes a monthly column entitled "Inside Track" that discusses the largest insider transactions. Security Analysts Several tests have considered whether it is possible to identify a set of analysts who have the ability to select undervalued stocks. The analysis involves determining whether, after a stock recommendation by an analyst is made known, a significant abnormal return is available to those who follow these recommendations. These studies and those that discuss performance by money managers are more realistic and relevant than those that considered corporate insiders because these analysts and money managers are full-time investment professionals with no obvious advantage except emphasis and training. If anyone should be able to select undervalued stocks, it should be these "pros." We initially examine Value Line rankings and then analyze the usefulness of recommendations by individual analysts. The Value Line Enigma Value Line (VL) is a large well-known advisory service that publishes financial information on approximately 1,700 stocks. Included in its report is a timing rank, which indicates Value Line's expectation regarding a firm's common stock performance over 166 Part 2: Developments in Investment Theory WWW.YAZDANPRESS.COM the coming 12 months. A rank of 1 is the most favorable performance metric and 5 is the worst. This ranking system, initiated in April 1965, assigns numbers based on four factors: 1. An earnings and price rank of each security relative to all others 2. A price momentum factor 3. Year-to-year relative changes in quarterly earnings 4. A quarterly earnings "surprise" factor (actual quarterly earnings compared with VL estimated earnings) The firms are ranked based on a composite score for each firm. The top and bottom 100 are ranked 1 and 5, respectively; the next 300 from the top and bottom are ranked 2 and 4; and the rest (approximately 900) are ranked 3. Rankings are assigned every week based on the latest data. Notably, all the data used to derive the four factors are public information. Several years after the ranking was started, Value Line contended that the stocks rated 1 substantially outperformed the market and the stocks rated 5 seriously underperformed the market (the performance figures did not include dividend income but also did not charge commissions). Early studies on the Value Line enigma indicated that there was information in the VL rankings (especially either rank 1 or 5) and in changes in the rankings (especially going from 2 to 1). Recent evidence indicates that the market is fairly efficient, because the abnormal adjustments appear to be complete by Day + 2. An analysis of study results over time likewise indicates a faster adjustment to the rankings during recent years. Also, despite statistically significant price changes, some evidence indicates that it is not possible to derive abnormal returns from these announcements after considering pre-2006 transaction costs. As before, it would be informative to reconsider those results with current transaction costs. The strongest evidence regarding not being able to use this information is that Value Line's Centurion Fund, which concentrates on investing in rank-1 stocks, has typically underperformed the market. Analysts' Recommendations There is evidence in favor of the existence of superior analysts who apparently possess private information. A study by Womack (1996) found that analysts appear to have both market timing and stock-picking ability, especially in connection with relatively rare sell recommendations. Jegadeesh et al. (2004) found that consensus recommendations do not contain incremental information for most stocks beyond other available signals (momentum and volume), but changes in consensus recommendations are useful. Alternatively, research by Ivkovic and Jegadeesh (2004) indicated that the most useful information consisted of upward earning revisions in the week prior to earnings announcements. A recent study by Goff, Hulbart, Keasler, and Walsh (2008) examined the information content of analyst recommendations after the passage of Regulation Fair Disclosure (REGFD) and concluded that recommendation changes continue to be informative. Performance of Professional Money Managers The studies of professional money managers are more realistic and widely applicable than the analysis of insiders because money managers typically do not have monopolistic access to important new information but are highly trained professionals who work full time at investment management. Therefore, if any "normal" set of investors should be able to derive above-average profits, it should be this group. Also, if any noninsider should be able to derive inside information, professional money managers should, because they conduct extensive management interviews and they may have the benefit of input from some superior analysts noted above. Most studies on the performance of money managers have examined mutual funds because performance data are readily available for them. Recently, data have become available for bank trust departments, insurance companies, and investment advisers. The original mutual fund studies indicated that most funds did not match the performance of a buy-and-hold policy When risk-adjusted returns were examined without considering commission costs, slightly more than half of the money managers did better than the overall market. When commission costs, load fees, and management costs were considered, approximately two-thirds of the mutual funds did not match aggregate market performance. It was also found that successful funds during individual years were inconsistent in their performance over time. Now that it is possible to get performance data for pension plans and endowment funds, several studies have documented that the performances of pension plans likewise did not match that of the aggregate market. The performance by endowments is interesting. Specifically, the results for a large sample of endowments confirm the inability to outperform the market. In contrast, the largest endowments in terms of size experienced superior risk-adjusted performance because of their ability and willingness to consider a wide variety of asset classes such as venture capital, unique hedge funds, real estate, and commodities on a global basis.

Our discussion up to this point has dealt with standard finance theory and how to test within this theoretical context whether capital markets are informationally efficient. However, in the 1990s, a new branch of financial economics was added to the mix. Behavioral finance considers how various psychological traits affect how individuals or groups act as investors, analysts, and portfolio managers. As noted by Olsen (1998), behavioral finance advocates recognize that the standard finance model of rational behavior and profit maximization can be true within specific boundaries, but they assert that it is an incomplete model since it does not consider individual behavior. It is argued that some financial phenomena can be better explained using models where it is recognized that some investors are not fully rational or realize that it is not possible for arbitrageurs to offset all instances of mispricing (Barberis and Thaler, 2003). Specifically, according to Olsen (1998), behavioral finance seeks to understand and predict systematic financial market implications of psychological decisions processes ... behavioral finance is focused on the implication of psychological and economic principles for the improvement of financial decision-making. (p. 11) In the preface for Wood (2010), the editor provides a helpful description of behavioral finance, alluding to a river with three tributaries that form the river of behavioral finance: (1) psychology that focuses on individual behavior, (2) social psychology, which is the study of how we behave and make decisions in the presence of others, and (3) neurofinance, which is the anatomy, mechanics, and functioning of the brain. It is contended that the goal of research in this area is to help us understand how and why we make choices. While it is still being debated whether there is a unified theory of behavioral finance, the emphasis has been twofold. First, on identifying portfolio anomalies that can be explained by various psychological traits in individuals and, second, identifying groups or pinpointing instances when it is possible to experience above-normal rates of return by exploiting the biases of investors, analysts, or portfolio managers. 6.4.1 Explaining Biases Over time it has been noted that investors have a number of biases that negatively affect their investment performance. Advocates of behavioral finance have been able to explain a number of these biases based on psychological characteristics. One major bias documented by Scott, Stumpp, and Xu (1999) is the propensity of investors to hold on to "losers" too long and sell "winners" too soon. Apparently, investors fear losses much more than they value gains—a tendency toward loss aversion. This aversion is explained by prospect theory, which contends that utility depends on deviations from moving reference points rather than absolute wealth. There are two related biases that seriously impact analysis and investment decisions. The first is belief perseverance, which means that once people have formed an opinion (on a company or stock) they cling to it too tightly and for too long. As a result, they are reluctant to search for contradictory beliefs, and even when they find such evidence, they are very skeptical about it or even misinterpret such information. A related bias is anchoring, wherein individuals who are asked to estimate something, start with an initial arbitrary (casual) value and then adjust away from it. The problem is that the adjustment is often insufficient. Therefore, if your initial estimate is low, you may raise it with information, but it is likely you will not raise it enough and thus will still end up below the "best estimates." Another bias documented by Solt and Statman (1989) and Shefrin and Statman (1996) for growth companies is overconfidence in forecasts, which causes analysts to overestimate the rates of growth and its duration for growth companies and overemphasize good news and ignore negative news for these firms. Analysts and many investors also suffer from representativeness, which causes them to believe that the stocks of growth companies will be "good" stocks. This bias is also referred to as confirmation bias, whereby investors look for information that supports prior opinions and decisions they have made. They also experience sample size neglect wherein they are prone to extrapolate the high growth results from a few past years (e.g., 4–6 years) for long-term periods. As a result, they will misvalue the stocks of these generally popular companies. Overconfidence is also related to self-attribution bias where people have a tendency to ascribe any success to their own talents while blaming any failure on "bad luck," which causes them to overestimate their talent (Gervais and Odean, 2001). Overconfidence is also nurtured by hindsight bias, which is a tendency after an event for an individual to believe that he or she predicted it, which causes people to think that they can predict better than they can. A study by Brown (1999) examined the effect of noise traders (nonprofessionals with no special information) on the volatility of closed-end mutual funds. When there is a shift in sentiment, these traders move together, which increases the prices and the volatility of these securities during trading hours. Also, Clarke and Statman (1998) find that noise traders tend to follow newsletter writers, who in turn tend to "follow the herd." These writers and "the herd" are almost always wrong, which contributes to excess volatility. Shefrin (2001) describes escalation bias, which causes investors to put more money into a failure that they feel responsible for rather than into a success. This leads to the relatively popular investor practice of "averaging down" on an investment that has declined in value since the initial purchase rather than consider selling the stock if it was a mistake. The thinking is that if it was a buy at $40, it is a screaming bargain at $30. Obviously, an alternative solution is to reevaluate the stock to see if some important bad news was missed in the initial valuation 170 Part 2: Developments in Investment Theory WWW.YAZDANPRESS.COM (therefore, sell it and accept the loss), or to confirm the initial valuation and acquire more of the "bargain." The difficult psychological factor noted by Shefrin (1999) is that you must seriously look for the bad news and consider the negative effects of this news on the valuation. 6.4.2 Fusion Investing According to Charles Lee (2003), fusion investing is the integration of two elements of investment valuation—fundamental value and investor sentiment. In Robert Shiller's (1984) formal model, the market price of securities is the expected dividends discounted to infinity (its fundamental value) plus a term that indicates the demand from noise traders who reflect investor sentiment. It is contended that when noise traders are bullish, stock prices will be higher than normal or higher than what is justified by fundamentals. Under this combination pricing model of fusion investing, investors will engage in fundamental analysis but also should consider investor sentiment in terms of fads and fashions. During some periods, investor sentiment is rather muted and noise traders are inactive, so that fundamental valuation dominates market returns. In other periods, when investor sentiment is strong, noise traders are very active and market returns are more heavily impacted by investor sentiments. Both investors and analysts should be cognizant of these dual effects on the aggregate market, various economic sectors, and individual stocks. Beyond advocating awareness of the dual components of fusion investing, results from other studies have documented that fundamental valuation may be the dominant factor but it takes much longer to assert itself—about three years. To derive some estimate of changing investor sentiment, Lee proposes several measures of investor sentiment, most notably analysts' recommendations, price momentum, and high trading turnover. Significant changes in these variables for a stock will indicate a movement from a glamour stock to a neglected stock or vice versa. The market price of a glamour stock will exceed its intrinsic value while a neglected stock will sell at a discount to its intrinsic value. 6.5 IMPLICATIONS OF EFFICIENT CAPITAL MARKETS Having reviewed the results of numerous studies related to different facets of the EMH, the important question is: What does this mean to individual investors, financial analysts, portfolio managers, and institutions? Overall, the results of many studies indicate that the capital markets are efficient as related to numerous sets of information. At the same time, research has uncovered a substantial number of instances where the market fails to adjust prices rapidly to public information. Given these mixed results regarding the existence of efficient capital markets, it is important to consider the implications of this contrasting evidence of market efficiency. The following discussion considers the implications of both sets of evidence. Specifically given results that support the EMH, we consider what techniques will not work and what you should do if you cannot beat the market. In contrast, because of the evidence that fails to support the EMH, we discuss what information and psychological biases should be considered when attempting to derive superior investment results through active security valuation and portfolio management. 6.5.1 Efficient Markets and Technical Analysis The assumptions of technical analysis directly oppose the notion of efficient markets. A basic premise of technical analysis is that stock prices move in trends that persist.11 Technicians believe that when new information comes to the market, it is not immediately available to everyone but is typically disseminated from the informed professional to the aggressive investing public and then to the great bulk of investors.

Also, technicians contend that investors do not analyze information and act immediately. This process takes time. Therefore, they hypothesize that stock prices move to a new equilibrium after the release of new information in a gradual manner, which causes trends in stock price movements that persist. Technical analysts believe that nimble traders can develop systems to detect the beginning of a movement to a new equilibrium (called a "breakout"). Hence, they hope to buy or sell the stock immediately after its breakout to take advantage of the subsequent, gradual price adjustment. The belief in this pattern of price adjustment directly contradicts advocates of the EMH who believe that security prices adjust to new information very rapidly. These EMH advocates do not contend, however, that prices adjust perfectly, which implies a chance of overadjustment or underadjustment. Still, because it is uncertain whether the market will over- or under-adjust at any time, you cannot derive abnormal profits from adjustment errors. If the capital market is weak-form efficient as indicated by most of the results, then prices fully reflect all relevant market information so technical trading systems that depend only on past trading data cannot have any value. By the time the information is public, the price adjustment has taken place. Therefore, a purchase or sale using a technical trading rule should not generate abnormal returns after taking account of risk and transaction costs. Still, recall the discussion in Chapter 4 regarding the dramatic decline in transaction costs due to the increase in trade volume and the significant new technology. Given this new environment, it is important to acknowledge that prior results that depended heavily on high transaction costs need to be reconsidered. 6.5.2 Efficient Markets and Fundamental Analysis As you know from our prior discussion, fundamental analysts believe that, at any time, there is a basic intrinsic value for the aggregate stock market, various industries, or individual securities and that these values depend on underlying economic factors. Therefore, investors should determine the intrinsic value of an investment asset at a point in time by examining the variables that determine value such as future earnings or cash flows, interest rates, and risk variables. If the prevailing market price differs from the estimated intrinsic value by enough to cover transaction costs, you should take appropriate action: You buy if the market price is substantially below intrinsic value and do not buy, or you sell, if the market price is above the intrinsic value. Investors who are engaged in fundamental analysis believe that, occasionally, market price and intrinsic value differ but eventually investors recognize the discrepancy and correct it. An investor who can do a superior job of estimating intrinsic value can consistently make superior market timing (asset allocation) decisions or acquire undervalued securities and generate above-average returns. Fundamental analysis involves aggregate market analysis, industry analysis, company analysis, and portfolio management. The divergent results from the EMH research have important implications for all of these components. Aggregate Market Analysis with Efficient Capital Markets Chapter 11 makes a strong case that intrinsic value analysis should begin with aggregate market analysis. Still, the EMH implies that if you examine only past economic events, it is unlikely that you will outperform a buy-and-hold policy because the market rapidly adjusts to known economic events. Evidence suggests that the market experiences long-run price movements; but, to take advantage of these movements in an efficient market, you must do a superior job of estimating the relevant variables that cause these long-run movements. Put another way, if you only use historical data to estimate future values and invest on the basis of these "old news" estimates, you will not experience superior, risk-adjusted returns. Industry and Company Analysis with Efficient Capital Markets As we discuss in Chapter 13, the wide distribution of returns from different industries and from different companies in an industry clearly justifies industry and company analysis. Again, the EMH 172 Part 2: Developments in Investment Theory WWW.YAZDANPRESS.COM does not contradict the potential value of such analysis but implies that you need to (1) understand the relevant variables that affect rates of return, and (2) do a superior job of estimating future values for these relevant valuation variables. To demonstrate this, Malkiel and Cragg (1970) developed a model that did an excellent job of explaining past stock price movements using historical data. When this valuation model was employed to project future stock price changes using past company data, however, the results were consistently inferior to a buyand-hold policy. This implies that, even with a good valuation model, you cannot select stocks that will provide superior future returns using only past data as inputs. The point is, most analysts are aware of the several well-specified valuation models, so the factor that differentiates superior from inferior analysts is the ability to provide more accurate estimates of the critical inputs to the valuation models and be different from the consensus. A study by Benesh and Peterson (1986) showed that the crucial difference between the stocks that enjoyed the best and worst price performance during a given year was the relationship between expected earnings of professional analysts and actual earnings (that is, it was earnings surprises). Specifically, stock prices increased if actual earnings substantially exceeded expected earnings and stock prices fell if actual earnings were below expected levels. As suggested by Fogler (1993), if you can do a superior job of projecting earnings and your expectations differ from the consensus (i.e., you project earnings surprises), you will have a superior stock selection record. To summarize this discussion, there are two factors that are required to be a superior analyst: (1) you must be correct in your estimates, and (2) you must be different from the consensus. Remember, if you are only correct and not different, that assumes you were predicting the consensus and the consensus was correct, which implies no surprise and no abnormal price movement. The quest to be a superior analyst holds some good news and some suggestions. The good news is related to the strong-form tests that indicated the likely existence of superior analysts. It was shown that the rankings by Value Line contained information value, even though it might not be possible to profit from the work of these analysts after transaction costs. Also, the price adjustments to the publication of analyst recommendations also point to the existence of superior analysts. The point is, there are some superior analysts, but only a limited number, and it is not an easy task to be among this select group. Most notably, to be a superior analyst you must do a superior job of estimating the relevant valuation variables and predicting earnings surprises, which implies that you differ from the consensus, then you should consistently identify undervalued or overvalued securities. The suggestions for those involved in fundamental analysis are based on the studies that considered the cross section of future returns. As noted, these studies indicated that P/E ratios, size, and the BV/MV ratios were able to differentiate future return patterns with size and the BV/MV ratio appearing to be the optimal combination. Therefore, these factors should be considered when selecting a universe or analyzing firms. In addition, the evidence suggests that neglected firms should be given extra consideration. Although these ratios and characteristics have been shown to be useful in isolating superior stocks from a large sample, it is our suggestion that they are best used to derive a viable sample to analyze from the total universe (e.g., select 200 stocks to analyze from a universe of 3,000). Then the 200 stocks should be rigorously valued using the techniques discussed in subsequent chapters. How to Evaluate Analysts or Investors If you want to determine if an individual is a superior analyst or investor, you should examine the performance of numerous securities that this analyst or investor recommends over time in relation to the performance of a set of randomly selected stocks of the same risk class. The stock selections of a superior analyst or investor should consistently outperform the randomly selected stocks. The consistency requirement is crucial because you would expect a portfolio developed by random selection to outperform the market about half the time.

Conclusions about Fundamental Analysis A text on investments can indicate the relevant variables that you should analyze and describe the important analysis techniques, but actually estimating the relevant variables is as much an art and a product of hard work as it is a science. If the estimates could be done on the basis of some mechanical formula, you could program a computer to do it, and there would be no need for analysts. Therefore, the superior analyst or successful investor must understand what variables are relevant to the valuation process and have the ability and work ethic to do a superior job of estimating values for these important valuation variables. There is no magic formula for superior estimation. Many times it simply means digging deeper and wider in your analysis to derive a better understanding of the economy, the industry and the firm. Alternatively, one can be superior if he or she has the ability to interpret the impact or estimate the effect of some public information better than others due to this better understanding. 6.5.3 Efficient Markets and Portfolio Management As noted, studies have indicated that the majority of professional money managers cannot beat a buy-and-hold policy on a risk-adjusted basis. One explanation for this generally inferior performance is that there are no superior analysts and the cost of research and trading forces the results of merely adequate analysis into the inferior category. Another explanation, which is favored by the authors and has some empirical support from the Value Line and analyst recommendation results, is that money management firms employ both superior and inferior analysts and the gains from the recommendations by the few superior analysts are offset by the costs and the poor results derived from the recommendations of the inferior analysts. This raises the question: Should a portfolio be managed actively or passively? The following discussion indicates that the decision of how to manage the portfolio (actively or passively) depends on whether the manager (or an investor) has access to superior analysts. A portfolio manager with superior analysts or an investor who believes that he or she has the time and expertise to be a superior investor can manage a portfolio actively by looking for undervalued or overvalued securities and trading accordingly. In contrast, without access to superior analysts or the time and ability to be a superior investor, you should manage passively and assume that all securities are properly priced based on their levels of risk. Portfolio Management with Superior Analysts A portfolio manager with access to superior analysts who have unique insights and analytical ability should follow their recommendations. The superior analysts should make investment recommendations for a certain proportion of the portfolio, and the portfolio manager should ensure that the risk preferences of the client are maintained. Also, the superior analysts should be encouraged to concentrate their efforts in mid-cap and small-cap stocks that possess the liquidity required by institutional portfolio managers. But because these stocks typically do not receive the attention given the top-tier stocks, the markets for these neglected stocks may be less efficient than the market for large well-known stocks that are being analyzed by numerous analysts. Recall that capital markets are expected to be efficient because many investors receive new information and analyze its effect on security values. If the number of analysts following a stock differ, one could conceive of differences in the efficiency of the markets. New information on top-tier stocks is well publicized and rigorously analyzed so the price of these securities should adjust rapidly to reflect the new information. In contrast, mid-cap and small-cap stocks receive less publicity and fewer analysts follow these firms, so prices may differ from intrinsic value for one of two reasons. First, because of less publicity, there is less information available on these firms. Second, there are fewer analysts following these firms so the adjustment to the new information is slowed. Therefore, the possibility of finding temporarily undervalued securities among these neglected stocks is greater. Again, in line with the cross-section study 174 Part 2: Developments in Investment Theory WWW.YAZDANPRESS.COM results, these superior analysts should pay particular attention to the BV/MV ratio, to the size of stocks being analyzed, and to the monetary policy environment. Portfolio Management without Superior Analysts A portfolio manager (or investor) who does not have access to superior analysts should proceed as follows. First, he or she should measure the risk preferences of his or her clients, then build a portfolio to match this risk level by investing a certain proportion of the portfolio in risky assets and the rest in a risk-free asset, as discussed in Chapter 8. The risky asset portfolio must be completely diversified on a global basis so it moves consistently with the world market. In this context, proper diversification means eliminating all unsystematic (unique) variability. In our prior discussion, it was estimated that it required about 20 securities to gain most of the benefits (more than 90 percent) of a completely diversified portfolio. More than 100 stocks are required for complete diversification. To decide how many securities to actually include in your global portfolio, you must balance the added benefits of complete worldwide diversification against the costs of research for the additional stocks. Finally, you should minimize transaction costs. Assuming that the portfolio is completely diversified and is structured for the desired risk level, excessive transaction costs that do not generate added returns will detract from your expected rate of return. Three factors are involved in minimizing total transaction costs: 1. Minimize taxes. Methods of accomplishing this objective vary, but it should receive prime consideration. 2. Reduce trading turnover. Trade only to sell overvalued stock out of the portfolio or add undervalued stock while maintaining a given risk level. 3. When you trade, minimize liquidity costs by trading relatively liquid stocks. To accomplish this, submit limit orders to buy or sell several stocks at prices that approximate the market-makers quote. That is, you would put in limit orders to buy stock at the bid price or sell at the ask price. The stock bought or sold first is the most liquid one; all other orders should be withdrawn. In summary, if you lack access to superior analysts, you should do the following: 1. Determine and quantify your risk preferences. 2. Construct the appropriate risk portfolio by dividing the total portfolio between risk-free assets and a risky asset portfolio. 3. Diversify completely on a global basis to eliminate all unsystematic risk. 4. Maintain the specified risk level by rebalancing when necessary. 5. Minimize total transaction costs. The Rationale and Use of Index Funds and Exchange-Traded Funds As discussed, efficient capital markets and a lack of superior analysts imply that many portfolios should be managed passively to match the performance of the aggregate market, minimizing the costs of research and trading. In response to this demand, several institutions have introduced index funds, which are security portfolios designed to duplicate the composition, and performance, of a selected market index series. Notably, this concept of stock-market index funds has been extended to other areas of investments and, as discussed by Gastineau (2001) and Kostovetsky (2003), has been enhanced by the introduction of exchange-traded funds (ETFs). Index bond funds attempt to emulate the bond-market indexes discussed in Chapter 5. Also, some index funds focus on specific segments of the market such as international bond-index funds, international stock-index funds that target specific countries, and index funds that target small-cap stocks in the United States and Japan. When financial planners want a given asset class in their portfolios, they often use Chapter 6: Efficient Capital Markets 175 WWW.YAZDANPRESS.COM index funds or ETFs to fulfill this need. Index funds or ETFs are less costly in terms of research and commissions, and, they generally provide the same or better performance than the majority of active portfolio managers. An innovation suggested by Arnott, Hsu, and West (2008) is to weight the stocks in an index fund based on fundamentals such as earnings, cash flow, and/or dividends rather than market values. Insights from Behavioral Finance As noted earlier, the major contributions of behavioral finance researchers are explanations for some of the anomalies discovered by prior academic research. They also suggest opportunities to derive abnormal rates of return by acting on some of the deeply ingrained biases of investors. For some further analysis, see Barbaris, Schliefer, and Vishney (1998). Clearly, their findings support the notion that the stocks of growth companies typically will not be growth stocks because analysts become overconfident in their ability to predict future growth rates and eventually derive valuations that either fully value or overvalue future growth. Behavioral finance research also supports the notion of contrary investing, confirming the notion of the herd mentality of analysts in stock recommendations or quarterly earning estimates and the recommendations by newsletter writers. Also, it is important to recall the loss aversion and escalation bias that causes investors to ignore bad news and hold losers too long and in some cases acquire additional shares of losers to average down the cost. Before averaging down, be sure you reevaluate the stock and consider all the potential bad news we tend to ignore. Finally, recognize that market prices are a combination of fundamental value and investor sentiment.

CHAPTER EIGHT

An Introduction to Portfolio Management

One of the major advances in the investment field during the past few decades has been the recognition that you cannot create an optimum investment portfolio by simply combining numerous individual securities that have desirable risk–return characteristics. Specifically, it has been shown that an investor must consider the relationship among the investments to build an optimum portfolio that will meet investment objectives. The recognition of how to create an optimum portfolio was demonstrated in the derivation of portfolio theory. In this chapter we explain portfolio theory in detail by introducing the basic portfolio risk formula for combining different assets. When you understand this formula and its implications, you will understand why and how you should diversify your portfolio. 7.1 SOME BACKGROUND ASSUMPTIONS We begin by clarifying some general assumptions of portfolio theory. This includes not only what we mean by an optimum portfolio but also what we mean by the terms risk aversion and risk. One basic assumption of portfolio theory is that investors want to maximize the returns from the total set of investments for a given level of risk. To understand such an assumption requires certain ground rules. First, your portfolio should include all of your assets and 181 WWW.YAZDANPRESS.COM liabilities, not only your marketable securities but also your car, house, and less marketable investments such as coins, stamps, art, antiques, and furniture. The full spectrum of investments must be considered because the returns from all these investments interact, and this relationship among the returns for assets in the portfolio is important. Hence, a good portfolio is not simply a collection of individually good investments. 7.1.1 Risk Aversion Portfolio theory also assumes that investors are basically risk averse, meaning that, given a choice between two assets with equal rates of return, they will select the asset with the lower level of risk. Evidence that most investors are risk averse is that they purchase various types of insurance, including life insurance, car insurance, and health insurance. Buying insurance basically involves an outlay of a known dollar value to guard against an uncertain, possibly larger, outlay in the future. Further evidence of risk aversion is the difference in promised yield (the required rate of return) for different grades of bonds with different degrees of credit risk. Specifically, the promised yield on corporate bonds increases from AAA (the lowest risk class) to AA to A, and so on, indicating that investors require a higher rate of return to accept higher risk. This does not imply that everybody is risk averse, or that investors are completely risk averse regarding all financial commitments. The fact is, not everybody buys insurance for everything. Some people have no insurance against anything, either by choice or because they cannot afford it. In addition, some individuals buy insurance related to some risks such as auto accidents or illness, but they also buy lottery tickets and gamble at race tracks or in casinos, where it is known that the expected returns are negative (which implies that participants are willing to pay for the excitement of the risk involved). This combination of risk preference and risk aversion can be explained by an attitude toward risk that depends on the amount of money involved. Researchers such as Friedman and Savage (1948) speculate that this is the case for people who like to gamble for small amounts (in lotteries or slot machines) but buy insurance to protect themselves against large losses such as fire or accidents. While recognizing such attitudes, we assume that most investors with a large investment portfolio are risk averse. Therefore, we expect a positive relationship between expected return and expected risk, which is consistent with the historical results shown in Chapter 3. 7.1.2 Definition of Risk Although there is a difference in the specific definitions of risk and uncertainty, for our purposes and in most financial literature the two terms are used interchangeably. For most investors, risk means the uncertainty of future outcomes. An alternative definition might be the probability of an adverse outcome. In our subsequent discussion of portfolio theory, we consider several measures of risk that are used when developing and applying the theory. 7.2 MARKOWITZ PORTFOLIO THEORY In the early 1960s, the investment community talked about risk, but there was no specific measure for the term. To build a portfolio model, however, investors had to quantify their risk variable. The basic portfolio model was developed by Harry Markowitz (1952, 1959), who derived the expected rate of return for a portfolio of assets and an expected risk measure. Markowitz showed that the variance of the rate of return was a meaningful measure of portfolio risk under a reasonable set of assumptions. More important, he derived the formula for computing the variance of a portfolio. This portfolio variance formula not only indicated the importance of diversifying investments to reduce the total risk of a portfolio but also showed 182 Part 2: Developments in Investment Theory WWW.YAZDANPRESS.COM how to effectively diversify. The Markowitz model is based on several assumptions regarding investor behavior: 1. Investors consider each investment alternative as being represented by a probability distribution of expected returns over some holding period. 2. Investors maximize one-period expected utility, and their utility curves demonstrate diminishing marginal utility of wealth. 3. Investors estimate the risk of the portfolio on the basis of the variability of expected returns. 4. Investors base decisions solely on expected return and risk, so their utility curves are a function of expected return and the expected variance (or standard deviation) of returns only. 5. For a given risk level, investors prefer higher returns to lower returns. Similarly, for a given level of expected return, investors prefer less risk to more risk. Under these assumptions, a single asset or portfolio of assets is considered to be efficient if no other asset or portfolio of assets offers higher expected return with the same (or lower) risk or lower risk with the same (or higher) expected return. 7.2.1 Alternative Measures of Risk One of the best-known measures of risk is the variance, or standard deviation of expected returns. 1 It is a statistical measure of the dispersion of returns around the expected value whereby a larger variance or standard deviation indicates greater dispersion. The idea is that the more dispersed the expected returns, the greater the uncertainty of future returns. Another measure of risk is the range of returns. It is assumed that a larger range of expected returns, from the lowest to the highest, means greater uncertainty regarding future expected returns. Instead of using measures that analyze all deviations from expectations, some observers believe that investors should be concerned only with returns below expectations, which means only deviations below the mean value. A measure that only considers deviations below the mean is the semivariance. An extension of the semivariance measure only computes expected returns below zero (that is, negative returns), or returns below the returns of some specific asset such as T-bills, the rate of inflation, or a benchmark. These measures of risk implicitly assume that investors want to minimize the damage (regret) from returns less than some target rate. Assuming that investors would welcome returns above some target rate, the returns above such a target rate are not considered when measuring risk. Although there are numerous potential measures of risk, we will use the variance or standard deviation of returns because (1) this measure is somewhat intuitive, (2) it is a correct and widely recognized risk measure, and (3) it has been used in most of the theoretical asset pricing models. 7.2.2 Expected Rates of Return We compute the expected rate of return for an individual investment as shown in Exhibit 7.1 and discussed in Chapter 1. The expected return for an individual risky asset with the set of potential returns and an assumption of the different probabilities used in the example would be 10.3 percent. The expected rate of return for a portfolio of investments is simply the weighted average of the expected rates of return for the individual investments in the portfolio. The weights are the proportion of total value for the individual investment.

CHAPTER NINE

An Introduction to Asset Pricing Models

Following the development of portfolio theory by Markowitz, two major theories have been derived for the valuation of risky assets. In this chapter, we introduce the first of these models—the capital asset pricing model (CAPM). The background on the CAPM is important at this point in the book because the risk measure it implies is a necessary input for much of our subsequent discussion. The presentation concerns capital market theory and the CAPM that was developed almost concurrently by three individuals. An alternative asset valuation model—the arbitrage pricing theory (APT)—has led to the development of numerous other multifactor models and is the subject of Chapter 9. 8.1 CAPITAL MARKET THEORY: AN OVERVIEW Because capital market theory builds directly on the portfolio theory we developed in Chapter 7, this chapter begins where our discussion of the Markowitz efficient frontier ended. In particular, capital market theory extends portfolio theory by developing a model for pricing all risky assets. The final product, the CAPM, will allow you to determine the required rate of return for any risky asset. As we will see, this development depends critically on the existence of a risk-free asset, which in turn will lead to the designation of the market portfolio, a collection of all of the risky assets in the marketplace that assumes a special role in asset pricing theory. 207 WWW.YAZDANPRESS.COM 8.1.1 Background for Capital Market Theory With any theory, it is necessary to articulate a set of assumptions that specify how the world is expected to act. In this section, we consider the main assumptions that underlie the development of capital market theory. Assumptions of Capital Market Theory Because capital market theory builds on the Markowitz portfolio model, it requires the same assumptions, along with some additional ones: 1. All investors are Markowitz-efficient in that they seek to invest in tangent points on the efficient frontier. The exact location of this tangent point and, therefore, the specific portfolio selected will depend on the individual investor's risk-return utility function. 2. Investors can borrow or lend any amount of money at the risk-free rate of return (RFR). (Clearly, it is always possible to lend money at the nominal risk-free rate by buying riskfree securities such as government T-bills. It is not always possible to borrow at this level.) 3. All investors have homogeneous expectations; that is, they estimate identical probability distributions for future rates of return. 4. All investors have the same one-period time horizon, such as one month or one year. The model will be developed for a single hypothetical period, and its results could be affected by a different assumption since it requires investors to derive risk measures and risk-free assets that are consistent with their investment horizons. 5. All investments are infinitely divisible, so it is possible to buy or sell fractional shares of any asset or portfolio. This assumption allows us to discuss investment alternatives as continuous curves. 6. There are no taxes or transaction costs involved in buying or selling assets. This is a reasonable assumption in many instances. Neither pension funds nor charitable foundations have to pay taxes, and the transaction costs for most financial institutions are negligible on most financial instruments. 7. There is no inflation or any change in interest rates, or inflation is fully anticipated. This is a reasonable initial assumption, and it can be modified. 8. Capital markets are in equilibrium. This means that we begin with all investments properly priced in line with their risk levels. Some of these assumptions may seem unrealistic, but keep in mind two things. First, as mentioned, relaxing them would have only a minor effect on the model and would not change its main implications or conclusions. Second, a theory should never be judged on the basis of its assumptions but rather on how well it explains and helps us predict behavior in the real world. If this theory and the model it implies help us explain the rates of return on a wide variety of risky assets, it is useful, even if some of its assumptions are unrealistic. Development of Capital Market Theory The major factor that allowed Markowitz portfolio theory to develop into capital market theory is the concept of a risk-free asset, that is, an asset with zero variance. As we will show, such an asset would have zero correlation with all other risky assets and would provide the risk-free rate of return (RFR). This assumption of a risk-free asset allows us to derive a generalized theory of capital asset pricing under conditions of uncertainty from the portfolio theory. This achievement is generally attributed to William Sharpe (1964), who received a Nobel Prize for it, but Lintner (1965) and Mossin (1966) derived similar theories independently. Consequently, you may see references to the Sharpe-Lintner-Mossin capital asset pricing model. 8.1.2 Developing the Capital Market Line We have defined a risky asset as one from which future returns are uncertain, and we have measured this uncertainty by the standard deviation of expected returns. Because the expected return on a risk-free asset is entirely certain, the standard deviation of its expected return is 208 Part 2: Developments in Investment Theory WWW.YAZDANPRESS.COM zero (σRF = 0). The rate of return earned on such an asset should be the risk-free rate of return (RFR), which, as we discussed in Chapter 1, should equal the expected long-run growth rate of the economy with an adjustment for short-run liquidity. We now show what happens when we introduce this risk-free asset into the risky world of the Markowitz portfolio model. Covariance with a Risk-Free Asset Recall that the covariance between two sets of returns is Covij = Xn i = 1 ½Ri − EðRiÞ½Rj − EðRjÞ=n Assume for the moment that asset i in this formula is the risk-free asset. Because the returns for the risk-free asset are certain (σRF = 0), Ri = E(Ri) during all periods. Thus, Ri − E(Ri) will equal zero, and the product of this expression with any other expression will equal zero. Consequently, the covariance of the risk-free asset with any risky asset or portfolio of assets will always equal zero. Similarly, the correlation between any risky asset i, and the risk-free asset, RF, would be zero because it is equal to rRF;i = CovRF;i=σRFσj Combining a Risk-Free Asset with a Risky Portfolio What happens to the expected rate of return and the standard deviation of returns when you combine a risk-free asset with a portfolio of risky assets such as those that exist on the Markowitz efficient frontier? Expected Return Like the expected return for a portfolio of two risky assets, the expected rate of return for a portfolio that includes a risk-free asset with a collection of risky assets (call it Portfolio M) is the weighted average of the two returns: EðRportÞ = wRFðRFRÞ + ð1 − wRFÞEðRMÞ where: wRF = the proportion of the portfolio invested in the risk-free asset EðRMÞ = the expected rate of return on risky Portfolio M Standard Deviation Recall from Chapter 7 that the expected variance for a two-asset portfolio is σ2 port = w2 1σ2 1 + w2 2σ2 2 + 2w1w2r1;2σ1σ2 Substituting the risk-free asset for Security 1, and the risky asset Portfolio M for Security 2, this formula would become σ2 port = w2 RFσ2 RF +

ð1 − wRFÞ 2 σ2 M + 2wRFð1 − wRFÞrRF;MσRFσM We know that the variance of the risk-free asset is zero, that is, σ2 RF = 0. Because the correlation between the risk-free asset and any risky asset, M, is also zero, the factor rRF,M in the preceding equation also equals zero. Therefore, any component of the variance formula that has either of these terms will equal zero. When you make these adjustments, the formula becomes σ2 port = ð1 − wRFÞ 2 σ2 M The standard deviation is σport = ffiffiffiffiffiffiffiffiffiffiffiffiffiffiffiffiffiffiffiffiffiffiffiffiffiffiffiffiffiffiffiffiffiffiffiffiffiffiffiffiffiffiffiffiffiffi ð1 − wRFÞ 2 σ2 M q = ð1 − wRFÞσM Therefore, the standard deviation of a portfolio that combines the risk-free asset with risky assets is the linear proportion of the standard deviation of the risky asset portfolio. Chapter 8: An Introduction to Asset Pricing Models 209 WWW.YAZDANPRESS.COM The Risk-Return Combination With these results, we can develop the risk-return relationship between E(Rport) and σport by using a few algebraic manipulations: EðRportÞ = ðwRFÞðRFRÞ + ð1 − wRFÞEðRMÞ + fRFR − RFRg = RFR − ð1 − wRFÞRFR + ð1 − wRFÞEðRMÞ = RFR + ð1 − wRFÞ½EðRMÞ − RFR = RFR + ð1 − wRFÞfσM=σMg½EðRMÞ − RFR so that 8.1 EðRportÞ = RFR + σport EðRMÞ − RFR σM Equation 8.1 is the primary result of capital market theory. It can be interpreted as follows: Investors who allocate their money between a riskless security and the risky Portfolio M can expect a return equal to the risk-free rate plus compensation for the number of risk units (σport) they accept. This outcome is consistent with the concept underlying all of investment theory that investors perform two functions in the capital markets for which they can expect to be rewarded. First, they allow someone else to use their money, for which they receive the risk-free rate of interest. Second, they bear the risk that the returns they have been promised in exchange for their invested capital will not be repaid. The term, ½EðRMÞ − RFR=σM, is the expected compensation per unit of risk taken, which is more commonly referred to as the investor's expected risk premium per unit of risk. The Capital Market Line The risk-return relationship shown in Equation 8.1 holds for every combination of the risk-free asset with any collection of risky assets. However, investors would obviously like to maximize their expected compensation for bearing risk (i.e., they would like to maximize the risk premium they receive). Let us now assume that Portfolio M is the single collection of risky assets that happens to maximize this risk premium. With this assumption, Portfolio M is called the market portfolio and, by definition, it contains all risky assets held anywhere in the marketplace and receives the highest level of expected return (in excess of the risk-free rate) per unit of risk for any available portfolio of risky assets. Under these conditions, Equation 8.1 is called the capital market line (CML). Exhibit 8.1 shows the various possibilities when a risk-free asset is combined with alternative risky combinations of assets along the Markowitz efficient frontier. Each of the straight lines depicted represents mixtures of a risky portfolio with the riskless asset. For instance, the risk-free asset could be combined in various weights with Portfolio A, as shown by the straight line RFR–A. Any combination on this line would dominate portfolio possibilities that fall below it because it would have a higher expected return for the same level of risk. Similarly, any combination of the risk-free asset and Portfolio A is dominated by some mixture of the riskfree asset and Portfolio B. You can continue to draw lines from RFR to the efficient frontier with increasingly higher slopes until you reach the point of tangency at Portfolio M. The set of portfolio possibilities along Line RFR–M—which is the CML—dominates all other feasible combinations that investors could form. For example, Point C could be established by investing half of your assets in the riskless security (i.e., lending at RFR) and the other half in Portfolio M. Notice in Exhibit 8.1 that there is no way to invest your money and achieve a higher expected return for the same level of risk (σc). In this sense, the CML represents a new efficient frontier that combines the Markowitz efficient frontier of risky assets with the ability to invest in the riskfree security. The slope of the CML is ½EðRMÞ – RFR=σM, which is the maximum risk premium compensation that investors can expect for each unit of risk they bear. 210 Part 2: Developments in Investment Theory WWW.YAZDANPRESS.COM Risk-Return Possibilities with Leverage An investor may want to attain a higher expected return than is available at Point M in exchange for accepting higher risk. One alternative would be to invest in one of the risky asset portfolios on the Markowitz frontier beyond Point M such as the portfolio at Point D. A second alternative is to add leverage to the portfolio by borrowing money at the risk-free rate and investing the proceeds in the risky asset portfolio at Point M; this is depicted as Point E. What effect would this have on the return and risk for your portfolio? If you borrow an amount equal to 50 percent of your original wealth at the risk-free rate, wRF will not be a positive fraction but, rather, a negative 50 percent (wRF = −0.50). The effect on the expected return for your portfolio is: EðRportÞ = wRFðRFRÞ + ð1 – wRFÞEðRMÞ = – 0:50ðRFRÞ + ½1 – ð−0:50ÞEðRMÞ

= − 0:50ðRFRÞ + 1:50EðRMÞ The return will increase in a linear fashion along the CML because the gross return increases by 50 percent, but you must pay interest at the RFR on the money borrowed. If RFR = 0.06 and E(RM) = 0.12, the return on your leveraged portfolio would be: EðRportÞ = − 0:50ð0:06Þ + 1:5ð0:12Þ = − 0:03 + 0:18 = 0:15 The effect on the standard deviation of the leveraged portfolio is similar. σport = ð1 − wRFÞσM = ½1 − ð−0:50ÞσM = 1:50σM where: σM = the standard deviation of Portfolio M Exhibit 8.1 Portfolio Possibilities Combining the Risk-Free Asset and Risky Portfolios on the Efficient Frontier C B A M D E Markowitz Efficient Frontier CML σC σM σE σport E(Rport) RFR Chapter 8: An Introduction to Asset Pricing Models 211 WWW.YAZDANPRESS.COM Therefore, both return and risk increase in a linear fashion along the CML. This is shown in Exhibit 8.2. Our discussion of portfolio theory stated that, when two assets are perfectly correlated, the set of portfolio possibilities falls along a straight line. Therefore, because the CML is a straight line, it implies that all the portfolios on the CML are perfectly positively correlated. This occurs because all portfolios on the CML combine the risky asset Portfolio M and the risk-free asset. You either invest part of your money in the risk-free asset (i.e., you lend at the RFR) and the rest in the risky asset Portfolio M, or you borrow at the risk-free rate and invest these funds in the risky asset portfolio. In either case, all the variability comes from the risky asset M portfolio. The only difference between the alternative portfolios on the CML is the magnitude of that variability, which is caused by the proportion of the risky asset portfolio held in the total portfolio. 8.1.3 Risk, Diversification, and the Market Portfolio The investment prescription that emerges from capital market theory is clear-cut: Investors should only invest their funds in two types of assets—the risk-free security and risky asset Portfolio M—with the weights of these two holdings determined by the investors' tolerance for risk. Because of the special place that the market Portfolio M holds for all investors, it must contain all risky assets for which there is any value in the marketplace. This includes not just U.S. common stocks, but also non-U.S. stocks, U.S. and non-U.S. bonds, real estate, private equity, options and futures contracts, art, antiques, and so on. Further, these assets should be represented in Portfolio M in proportion to their relative market values. Since the market portfolio contains all risky assets, it is a completely diversified portfolio, which means that all risk unique to individual assets in the portfolio is diversified away. Unique risk—which is often called unsystematic risk—of any single asset is offset by the unique variability of all of the other holdings in the portfolio. This implies that only systematic risk, defined as the variability in all risky assets caused by macroeconomic variables, remains in Portfolio M. Systematic risk can be measured by the standard deviation of returns to the market portfolio, and it changes over time whenever there are changes in the underlying economic forces that affect the valuation of all risky assets, such as variability of Exhibit 8.2 Derivation of Capital Market Line Assuming Lending or Borrowing at the Risk-Free Rate CML Borrowing Lending M σport E(Rport) RFR 212 Part 2: Developments in Investment Theory WWW.YAZDANPRESS.COM money supply growth, interest rate volatility, and variability in industrial production or corporate earnings.1 How to Measure Diversification We have seen that all portfolios on the CML are perfectly positively correlated, so all portfolios on the CML are perfectly correlated with the completely diversified market Portfolio M. Lorie (1975) notes that a completely diversified portfolio would have a correlation with the market portfolio of +1.00. This is logical because complete diversification means the elimination of all the unsystematic or unique risk. Once this occurs, only systematic risk is left, which cannot be diversified away. Therefore, completely diversified portfolios would correlate perfectly with the market portfolio, which has only systematic risk. Diversification and the Elimination of Unsystematic Risk As discussed in Chapter 7, the purpose of diversification is to reduce the standard deviation of the total portfolio. This assumes imperfect correlations among securities. Ideally, as you add securities, the average covariance for the portfolio declines. How many securities must be included to arrive at a completely diversified portfolio? For the answer, you must observe what happens as you increase the sample size of the portfolio by adding securities that have some positive correlation. The typical correlation between U.S. securities ranges from 0.20 to 0.60. One set of studies examined the average standard deviation for numerous portfolios of randomly selected stocks of different sample sizes. Evans and Archer (1968) and Tole (1982) computed the standard deviation for portfolios of increasing size up to 20 stocks. The results indicated that the major benefits of diversification were achieved rather quickly, with about 90 percent of the maximum benefit of diversification derived from portfolios of 12 to 18 stocks. Exhibit 8.3 shows a stylized depiction of this effect. Two subsequent studies have modified this finding. Statman (1987) considered the trade-off between the diversification benefits and additional transaction costs involved with increasing the size of a portfolio.

He concluded that a well-diversified portfolio must contain at least Exhibit 8.3 Number of Stocks in a Portfolio and the Standard Deviation of Portfolio Return Number of Stocks in the Portfolio Standard Deviation of Return Standard Deviation of the Market Portfolio (Systematic Risk) 0.30 0.15 10 20 Systematic Risk Total Risk Unsystematic (Diversifiable) Risk 1 For analyses of changes in the standard deviation (volatility) of returns for stocks and bonds in the United States, see Schwert (1989); Ineichen (2000); Reilly, Wright, and Chan (2000); and Ang, Hodrick, Xing, and Zhang (2006). Chapter 8: An Introduction to Asset Pricing Models 213 WWW.YAZDANPRESS.COM 30–40 stocks. Campbell, Lettau, Malkiel, and Xu (2001) demonstrated that because the idiosyncratic portion of an individual stock's total risk has been increasing in recent years, it now takes more stocks in a portfolio to achieve the same level of diversification. For instance, they showed that the level of diversification that was possible with only 20 stocks in the 1960s would require about 50 stocks by the late 1990s. The important point is that, by adding stocks to a portfolio that are not perfectly correlated with stocks already held, you can reduce the overall standard deviation of the portfolio, which will eventually reach the level of the market portfolio. At that point, you will have diversified away all unsystematic risk, but you still have market or systematic risk. You cannot eliminate the variability and uncertainty of macroeconomic factors that affect all risky assets. Further, you can attain a lower level of systematic risk by diversifying globally versus only diversifying within the United States because some of the systematic risk factors in the U.S. market (such as U.S. monetary policy) are not perfectly correlated with systematic risk variables in other countries like Germany and Japan. As a result, if you diversify globally, you eventually get down to a world systematic risk level. The CML and the Separation Theorem The CML leads all investors to invest in the same risky asset Portfolio M. Individual investors should only differ regarding their position on the CML, which depends on their risk preferences. In turn, how they get to a point on the CML is based on their financing decisions. If you are relatively risk averse, you will lend some part of your portfolio at the RFR by buying some risk-free securities and investing the remainder in the market portfolio of risky assets (e.g., Point C in Exhibit 8.1). In contrast, if you prefer more risk, you might borrow funds at the RFR and invest everything (all of your capital plus what you borrowed) in the market portfolio (Point E in Exhibit 8.1). This financing decision provides more risk but greater expected returns than the market portfolio. Because portfolios on the CML dominate other portfolio possibilities, the CML becomes the efficient frontier of portfolios, and investors decide where they want to be along this efficient frontier. Tobin (1958) called this division of the investment decision from the financing decision the separation theorem. Specifically, to be somewhere on the CML efficient frontier, you initially decide to invest in the market Portfolio M. This is your investment decision. Subsequently, based on your risk preferences, you make a separate financing decision either to borrow or to lend to attain your preferred risk position on the CML. A Risk Measure for the CML In discussing the Markowitz portfolio model, we noted that the relevant risk to consider when adding a security to a portfolio is its average covariance with all other assets in the portfolio. In this chapter, we have shown that the only relevant portfolio is the market Portfolio M. Together, this means that the only important consideration for any individual risky asset is its average covariance with all the risky assets in Portfolio M or the asset's covariance with the market portfolio. This covariance, then, is the relevant risk measure for an individual risky asset. Because all individual risky assets are a part of the market portfolio, one can describe their rates of return in relation to the returns to Portfolio M using the following linear model: 8.2 Rit = ai + biRMt + ε where: Rit = return for asset i during period t ai = constant term for asset i bi = slope coefficient for asset i RMt = return for Portfolio M during period t ε = random error term 214 Part 2: Developments in Investment Theory WWW.YAZDANPRESS.COM The variance of returns for a risky asset can similarly be described as 8.3 VarðRitÞ =Varðai + biRMt + εÞ =VarðaiÞ +VarðbiRMtÞ +VarðεÞ = 0 +VarðbiRMtÞ +VarðεÞ Note that Var(biRMt) is the variance of return for an asset related to the variance of the market return, or the asset's systematic variance or risk. Also, Var(ε) is the residual variance of return for the individual asset that is not related to the market portfolio. This residual variance is what we have referred to as the unsystematic or unique risk because it arises from the unique features of the asset. Therefore: Var(Ri,t) = Systematic Variance + Unsystematic Variance We know that a completely diversified portfolio has had all of its unsystematic variance eliminated. Therefore, the unsystematic variance of an asset is not relevant to investors, because they can eliminate it when holding an asset as part of a broad-based portfolio. As a consequence, investors should not expect to receive compensation for bearing this unsystematic risk. Only the systematic variance is relevant because it cannot be diversified away. 8.1.4 Investing with the CML: An Example After doing considerable research on current capital market conditions, you have estimated the investment characteristics for six different combinations of risky assets. Exhibit 8.4 lists your expected return and standard deviation forecasts for these portfolios. You have also established that each of these portfolios is completely diversified so that its volatility estimate represents systematic risk only. The risk-free rate at the time of your analysis is 4 percent. Based on your forecasts for E(R) and σ alone, none of these portfolios clearly dominates the others since higher levels of expected return always come at the cost of higher levels of risk. Which portfolio offers the best trade-off between risk and return? The last column in Exhibit 8.4 calculates the ratio of the expected risk premium (E(R) – RFR) to volatility (σ) for each portfolio. As explained earlier, this ratio is the amount of compensation that investors can expect for each unit of risk they assume in a particular portfolio. For example, Portfolio 2 offers investors 0.429 (= [7 – 4]/7) units of compensation per unit of risk while the comparable ratio for Portfolio 6 is lower at 0.393 (= [15 – 4]/28), despite promising a much higher overall return. By this measure, Portfolio 3 offers investors the best combination of risk and return. No other feasible collection of risky assets in this comparison can match the 0.500 units of expected risk premium per unit of risk. Consequently, Portfolio 3 should be considered as the market portfolio. Capital market theory would recommend that you only consider two Exhibit 8.4 Investment Characteristics for Portfolios of Risky Assets (RFR = 4%) Portfolio Expected Return Standard Deviation [E (R) – RFR]/σ 1 5% 5% 0.200 2 7 7 0.429 3 9 10 0.500 4 11 15 0.467 5 13 21 0.429 6 15 28 0.393 Chapter 8: An Introduction to Asset Pricing Models 215 WWW.YAZDANPRESS.COM alternatives when investing your funds: (1) lending or borrowing in the riskless security at 4 percent, and (2) buying Portfolio 3. Suppose now that given your risk tolerance you are willing to assume a standard deviation of 8.5 percent. How should you go about investing your money, according to the CML? First, using Equation 8.1, the return you can expect is: 4% + (8.5%)(0.500) = 8.25% As we have seen, there is no way for you to obtain a higher expected return under the current conditions without assuming more risk. Second, the investment strategy necessary to achieve this return can be found by solving: 8.25% = wRF(4%) + (1 – wRF)(9%) or wRF = (9 – 8.25)/(9 – 4) = 0.15. This means that you would need to invest 15 percent of your funds in the riskless asset and the remaining 85 percent in Portfolio 3. Finally, notice that the expected risk premium per unit of risk for this position is 0.500 (= [8.25 – 4]/8.5), the same as Portfolio 3. In fact, all points along the CML will have the same risk-return trade-off as the market portfolio since this ratio is the slope of the CML. As a last extension, consider what would happen if you were willing to take on a risk level of σ = 15 percent. From Exhibit 8.4, you could realize an expected return of 11 percent if you placed 100 percent of funds in Portfolio 4. However, you can do better than this by following the investment prescription of the CML. Specifically, for a risk level of 15 percent, you can obtain an expected return of: 4% + (15%)(0.500) = 11.5% This goal is greater than the expected return offered by a 100 percent investment in the market portfolio (i.e., 9 percent), so you will have to use leverage to achieve it. Specifically, solving for the investment weights along the CML leaves wRF = (9 – 11.5)/(9 – 4) = −0.50 and (1 – wRF) = 1.50. Thus, for each dollar you currently have to invest, you will need to borrow an additional 50 cents and place all of these funds in Portfolio 3. 8.2 THE CAPITAL ASSET PRICING MODEL Capital market theory represented a major step forward in how investors should think about the investment process. The formula for the CML (Equation 8.1) offers a precise way of calculating the return that investors can expect for (1) providing their financial capital (RFR), and (2) bearing σport units of risk ([E(RM) – RFR]/σM). This last term is especially significant because it expresses the expected risk premium prevailing in the marketplace. Unfortunately, capital market theory is an incomplete explanation for the relationship that exists between risk and return. To understand why, recall that the CML defined the risk an investor bears by the total volatility (σ) of the investment. However, since investors cannot expect to be compensated for any portion of risk that they could have diversified away (i.e., unsystematic risk), the CML must be based on the assumption that investors only hold fully diversified portfolios, for which total risk and systematic risk are the same thing. The limitation is thus that the CML cannot provide an explanation for the risk-return trade-off for individual risky assets because the standard deviation for these securities will contain a substantial amount of unique risk. The capital asset pricing model (CAPM) extends capital market theory in a way that allows investors to evaluate the risk-return trade-off for both diversified portfolios and individual securities. To do this, the CAPM redefines the relevant measure of risk from total volatility to just the nondiversifiable portion of that total volatility (i.e., systematic risk). This new risk measure is called the beta coefficient, and it calculates the level of a security's systematic risk compared to that of the market portfolio. Using beta as the relevant measure of risk, the 216 Part 2: Developments in Investment Theory WWW.YAZDANPRESS.COM CAPM then redefines the expected risk premium per unit of risk in a commensurate fashion. This in turn leads once again to an expression of the expected return that can be decomposed into (1) the risk-free rate and (2) the expected risk premium. 8.2.1 A Conceptual Development of the CAPM As noted earlier, Sharpe (1964), along with Lintner (1965) and Mossin (1966), developed the CAPM in a formal way. In addition to the assumptions listed before, the CAPM requires others, such as that asset returns come from a Normal probability distribution. Rather than a mathematical derivation of the CAPM, we will present a conceptual development of the model, emphasizing its role in the natural progression that began with the Markowitz portfolio theory. Recall that the CML expressed the risk-return trade-off for fully diversified portfolios as follows: EðRportÞ = RFR + σport EðRMÞ − RFR σM When trying to extend this expression to allow for the evaluation of any individual risky asset i, the logical temptation is to simply replace the standard deviation of the portfolio (σport) with that of the single security (σi). However, this would overstate the relevant level of risk in the ith security because it does not take into account how much of that volatility the investor could diversify away by combining that asset with other holdings. One way to address this concern is to "shrink" the level of σi to include only the portion of risk in Security i that is systematically related to the risk in the market portfolio. This can be done by multiplying σi by the correlation coefficient between the returns to Security i and the market portfolio (riM). Inserting this product into the CML and adapting the notation for the ith individual asset leaves: EðRiÞ = RFR + ðσiriMÞ EðRMÞ − RFR σM This expression can be rearranged as: EðRiÞ = RFR + σiriM σM ½EðRMÞ − RFR or: 8.4 EðRiÞ = RFR + βi ½EðRMÞ − RFR: Equation 8.4 is the CAPM. The CAPM redefines risk in terms of a security's beta (βi), which captures the nondiversifiable portion of that stock's risk relative to the market as a whole. Because of this, beta can be thought of as indexing the asset's systematic risk to that of the market portfolio. This leads to a very convenient interpretation: A stock with a beta of 1.20 has a level of systematic risk that is 20 percent greater than the average for the entire market, while a stock with a beta of 0.70 is 30 percent less risky than the market. By definition, the market portfolio itself will always have a beta of 1.00. Indexing the systematic risk of an individual security to the market has another nice feature as well. From Equation 8.4, it is clear that the CAPM once again expresses the expected return for an investment as the sum of the risk-free rate and the expected risk premium. However, rather than calculate a different risk premium for every separate security that exists, the CAPM states that only the overall market risk premium (E(RM) - RFR) matters and that this quantity can then be adapted to any risky asset by scaling it up or down according to that asset's riskiness relative to the market (βi). As we will see, this substantially reduces the number of calculations that investors must make when evaluating potential investments for their portfolios. Chapter 8: An Introduction to Asset Pricing Models 217 WWW.YAZDANPRESS.COM 8.2.2 The Security Market Line The CAPM can also be illustrated in graphical form as the security market line (SML). This is shown in Exhibit 8.5. Like the CML, the SML shows the trade-off between risk and expected return as a straight line intersecting the vertical axis (i.e., zero-risk point) at the risk-free rate. However, there are two important differences between the CML and the SML. First, the CML measures risk by the standard deviation (i.e., total risk) of the investment while the SML considers only the systematic component of an investment's volatility. Second, as a consequence of the first point, the CML can be applied only to portfolio holdings that are already fully diversified, whereas the SML can be applied to any individual asset or collection of assets. Determining the Expected Rate of Return for a Risky Asset To demonstrate how you would compute expected or required rates of return with the CAPM, consider the following example stocks, assuming you have already computed betas: Stock Beta A 0.70 B 1.00 C 1.15 D 1.40 E −0.30 Assume that we expect the economy's RFR to be 5 percent (0.05) and the expected return on the market portfolio (E(RM)) to be 9 percent (0.09). This implies a market risk premium of 4 percent (0.04). With these inputs, the SML would yield the following required rates of return for these five stocks: EðRiÞ = RFR + βi ½EðRMÞ − RFR EðRAÞ = 0:05 + 0:70ð0:09 − 0:05Þ = 0:078 = 7:80% EðRBÞ = 0:05 + 1:00ð0:09 − 0:05Þ = 0:09 = 9:00% Exhibit 8.5 The Security Market Line 0 0.1 βi Negative Beta SML E(RM) RFR E(Ri) 218 Part 2: Developments in Investment Theory WWW.YAZDANPRESS.COM EðRCÞ = 0:05 + 1:15ð0:09 − 0:05Þ = 0:096 = 9:60% EðRDÞ = 0:05 + 1:40ð0:09 − 0:05Þ = 0:106 = 10:60% EðREÞ = 0:05 + ð− 0:30Þð0:09 − 0:05Þ = 0:05 −

0:012 = 0:038 = 3:80% Stock A has lower risk than the aggregate market, so you should not expect its return to be as high as the return on the market portfolio. You should expect Stock A to return 7.80 percent. Stock B has systematic risk equal to the market's (beta = 1.00), so its required rate of return should likewise be equal to the expected market return (9 percent). Stocks C and D have systematic risk greater than the market's, so they should provide returns consistent with their risk. Finally, Stock E has a negative beta (which is quite rare in practice), so its required rate of return, if such a stock could be found, would be below the RFR of 5 percent. In equilibrium, all assets and all portfolios of assets should plot on the SML. That is, all assets should be priced so that their estimated rates of return, which are the actual holding period rates of return that you anticipate, are consistent with their levels of systematic risk. Any security with an estimated rate of return that plots above the SML would be considered undervalued because it implies that you forecast receiving a rate of return on the security that is above its required rate of return based on its systematic risk. In contrast, assets with estimated rates of return that plot below the SML would be considered overvalued. This position relative to the SML implies that your estimated rate of return is below what you should require based on the asset's systematic risk. In an efficient market, you would not expect any assets to plot off the SML because, in equilibrium, all stocks should provide holding period returns that are equal to their required rates of return. Alternatively, a market that is not completely efficient may misprice certain assets because not everyone will be aware of all the relevant information. As discussed in Chapter 6, a superior investor has the ability to derive value estimates for assets that consistently outperform the consensus market evaluation. As a result, such an investor will earn better rates of return than the average investor on a risk-adjusted basis. Identifying Undervalued and Overvalued Assets Now that we understand how to compute the rate of return one should expect or require for a specific risky asset using the SML, we can compare this required rate of return to the asset'sestimated rate of return over a specific investment horizon to determine whether it would be an appropriate investment. To make this comparison, you need an independent estimate of the return outlook for the security based on either fundamental or technical analysis techniques, which will be discussed in subsequent chapters. Assume that analysts at a major brokerage firm have been following the five stocks in the preceding example. Based on extensive fundamental analysis, they provide you with forecasted price and dividend information for the next year, as shown in Exhibit 8.6. Given these projections, you can compute an estimated rate of return for each stock by summing the expected capital gain ([Pt+1 – Pt]/Pt) and the expected dividend yield (Dt+1/Pt). For example, the analysts' estimated future return for Stock A is 8.00 percent (= [26 – 25]/25 + 1/25). Exhibit 8.7 summarizes the relationship between the required rate of return for each stock based on its systematic risk as computed earlier, and its estimated rate of return. This difference between estimated return and expected return is sometimes referred to as a stock's expected alpha or its excess return. This alpha can be positive (the stock is undervalued) or negative (the stock is overvalued). If the alpha is zero (or nearly zero), the stock is on the SML and is properly valued in line with its systematic risk.

CHAPTER TEN

Multifactor Models of Risk and Return

The last chapter highlighted many of the ways in which the CAPM has contributed to the investment management field. In many respects, the CAPM has been one of the most useful— and frequently used—financial economic theories ever developed. However, some of the empirical studies cited point out deficiencies in the model as an explanation of the link between risk and return. For example, tests of the CAPM indicated that the beta coefficients for individual securities were not stable but that portfolio betas generally were stable. There was mixed support for a positive linear relationship between rates of return and systematic risk for portfolios of stock, with some recent evidence indicating the need to consider additional risk variables or a need for different risk proxies. In addition, other papers criticized the tests of the model and its usefulness in portfolio evaluation because of a dependence on a market portfolio that is not currently available. One major challenge to the CAPM was the set of results suggesting that it is possible to use knowledge of certain firm or security characteristics to develop profitable trading strategies, even after adjusting for investment risk as measured by beta. Banz (1981) showed that portfolios of stocks with low market capitalizations (i.e., "small" stocks) outperformed "large" stock portfolios on a risk-adjusted basis, and Basu (1977) documented that stocks with low priceearnings (P/E) ratios similarly outperformed high P/ E stocks. More recent work by Fama and French (1992) also demonstrated that "value" stocks (i.e., those with high book valueto-market price ratios) tend to produce larger risk-adjusted returns than "growth" stocks (i.e., those with low book-to-market ratios). In an efficient market, these return differentials should not occur, meaning that either: (1) markets are not particularly efficient for extended periods of time (i.e., investors have been ignoring profitable investment opportunities for decades), or (2) market prices are efficient, but there is something wrong with the way the single-factor models such as the CAPM measure risk. Given the implausibility of the first possibility, in the early 1970s financial economists began to consider the implications of the second. The academic community searched for an alternative asset pricing theory to the CAPM that was reasonably intuitive, required only limited assumptions, and allowed for multiple dimensions of investment risk. The result was the APT, which was developed by Ross (1976, 1977) in the mid-1970s and has three major assumptions: 1. Capital markets are perfectly competitive. 2. Investors always prefer more wealth to less wealth with certainty. 3. The stochastic process generating asset returns can be expressed as a linear function of a set of K risk factors (or indexes), and all unsystematic risk is diversified away.

www.ingramcontent.com/pod-product-compliance
Ingram Content Group UK Ltd.
Pitfield, Milton Keynes, MK11 3LW, UK
UKHW021910190726
13853UKWH00002B/601